EDITORIAL

IN THIS ISSUE:

ISSUE 07 JULY 2017

PUBLISHER
Tourism Tattler (Pty) Ltd.
PO Box 891, Umhlanga Rocks, 4320
KwaZulu-Natal, South Africa.
Website: www.tourismtattler.com

EXECUTIVE EDITOR Des Langkilde
Cell: +27 (0)82 374 7260
Fax: +27 (0)86 651 8080
E-mail: editor@tourismtattler.com
Skype: tourismtattler

MAGAZINE ADVERTISING
ADVERTISING DIRECTOR Bev Langkilde
Cell: +27 (0)71 224 9971
Fax: +27 (0)86 656 3860
E-mail: bev@tourismtattler.com
Skype: bevtourismtattler

SUBSCRIPTIONS
http://eepurl.com/bocldD

BACK ISSUES (Click on the covers below).

▼ JUN 2017 ▼ MAY 2017 ▼ APR 2017
 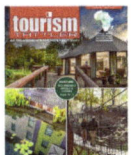 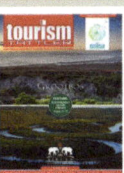

▼ MAR 2017 ▼ FEB 2017 ▼ JAN 2017
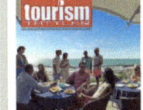  

▼ DEC 2016 ▼ NOV 2016 ▼ OCT 2016

▼ SEP 2016 ▼ AUG 2016 ▼ JUL 2016

CONTENTS

AFRICA: SUSTAINABLE TOURISM SOLUTIONS
- 07 Conscious Conferencing
- 08 Join Fair Trade To Move Toward Sustainability
- 09 Eco & Sustainable Tourism Icons

SOUTH AFRICA: ECO-FRIENDLY HOTELS & LODGES
- 10 Coffeebeans Routes
- 11 Parker Cottage
- 12 Spier

BUSINESS & FINANCE
- 13 Celebrating the Economic Impact of Lalibela
- 14 Economic Development in Africa
- 16 South African Tourism Statistics: Jan-May 2017
- 17 HVS Africa Hotel Valuation Index

CONSERVATION
- 24 A Ranger's View On Rhino Poaching

DESTINATIONS
- 26 Exploring Zanzibar

EVENTS
- 29 8 Reasons to Attend THINC Africa 2017

HOSPITALITY
- 30 Property Review: Town Lodge Midrand

LEGAL
- 31 The Consumer Goods & Services Ombudsman - Part 1

EDITORIAL CONTRIBUTORS
Des Langkilde   Martin Janse van Vuuren
Louis Nel

MAGAZINE SPONSORS
- 02 City Lodge Hotel Group
- 03 World Luxury Spa & Restaurant Awards
- 05 Bookings2Africa
- 06 ATA Congress Rwanda 2017
- 10 Coffeebeans Routes
- 11 Parker Cottage
- 12 Spier
- 13 Lalibela Private Game Reserve

SUPPORTED CHARITIES
- 32 Diabetes South Africa

Disclaimer: The Tourism Tattler is published by Tourism Tattler (Pty) Ltd and is the official trade journal of various trade 'associations' (see page 02). The Tourism Tattler digital e-zine, is distributed free of charge to bona fide tourism stakeholders. Letters to the Editor are assumed intended for publication in whole or part and may therefore be used for such purpose. The information provided and opinions expressed in this publication are provided in good faith and do not necessarily represent the opinions of Tourism Tattler (Pty) Ltd, its 'Associations', its staff and its production suppliers. Advice provided herein should not be soley relied upon as each set of circumstances may differ. Professional advice should be sought in each instance. Neither Tourism Tattler (Pty) Ltd, its 'Associations', its staff and its production suppliers can be held legally liable in any way for damages of any kind whatsoever arising directly or indirectly from any facts or information provided or omitted in these pages or from any statements made or withheld or from supplied photographs or graphic images reproduced by the publication.

"OK" WAS HIS FAVOURITE COMPLIMENT.

BUT OUR EXCLUSIVE CLUB LOUNGE EARNED A "VERY NICE".

COURTYARD HOTEL

DESIGNED TO IMPRESS.

FOR RATES AND RESERVATIONS, CALL 0800 11 37 90 OR VISIT WWW.CLHG.COM

EVENT MEDIA PARTNER

A celebration of the grandest service excellence in the luxury spa and restaurant industries. Signifying all things luxury, the JW Marriott Hotel Hanoi will play host to this glamorous occasion, as honours are received by the top wellness and fine dining establishments around the globe.

WORLD LUXURY SPA & RESTAURANT Awards

22 JULY 2017 | HANOI, VIETNAM

www.luxuryspaawards.com

www.luxuryrestaurantawards.com

JW MARRIOTT HANOI · WORLD LUXURY RESTAURANT AWARDS · WORLD LUXURY SPA AWARDS · THERAVINE SKIN SCIENCE

EDITORIAL

ACCREDITATION

Official Travel Trade Journal and Media Partner to:

The Africa Travel Association (ATA)
Tel: +1 212 447 1357 • Email: info@africatravelassociation.org • Website: www.africatravelassociation.org

ATA is a division of the Corporate Council on Africa (CCA), and a registered non-profit trade association in the USA, with headquarters in Washington, DC and chapters around the world. ATA is dedicated to promoting travel and tourism to Africa and strengthening intra-Africa partnerships. Established in 1975, ATA provides services to both the public and private sectors of the industry.

The African Travel & Tourism Association (Atta)
Tel: +44 20 7937 4408 • Email: info@atta.travel • Website: www.atta.travel

Members in 22 African countries and 37 worldwide use Atta to: Network and collaborate with peers in African tourism; Grow their online presence with a branded profile; Ask and answer specialist questions and give advice; and Attend key industry events.

National Accommodation Association of South Africa (NAA-SA)
Tel: +27 86 186 2272 • Fax: +2786 225 9858 • Website: www.naa-sa.co.za

The NAA-SA is a network of mainly smaller accommodation providers around South Africa – from B&Bs in country towns offering comfortable personal service to luxurious boutique city lodges with those extra special touches – you're sure to find a suitable place, and at the same time feel confident that your stay at an NAA-SA member's establishment will meet your requirements.

Regional Tourism Organisation of Southern Africa (RETOSA)
Tel: +27 11 315 2420/1 • Fax: +27 11 315 2422 • Website: www.retosa.co.za

RETOSA is a Southern African Development Community (SADC) institution responsible for tourism growth and development. RETOSA's aims are to increase tourist arrivals to the region through. RETOSA Member States are Angola, Botswana, DR Congo, Lesotho, Madagascar, Malawi, Mauritius, Mozambique, Namibia, Seychelles, South Africa, Swaziland, Tanzania, Zambia and Zimbabwe.

Southern African Vehicle Rental and Leasing Association (SAVRALA)
Contact: manager@savrala.co.za • Website: www.savrala.co.za

Founded in the 1970's, SAVRALA is the representative voice of Southern Africa's vehicle rental, leasing and fleet management sector. Our members have a combined national footprint with more than 600 branches countrywide. SAVRALA are instrumental in steering industry standards and continuously strive to protect both their members' interests, and those of the public, and are therefore widely respected within corporate and government sectors.

Seychelles Hospitality & Tourism Association (SHTA)
Tel: +248 432 5560 • Fax: +248 422 5718 • Website: www.shta.sc

The Seychelles Hospitality and Tourism Association was created in 2002 when the Seychelles Hotel Association merged with the Seychelles Hotel and Guesthouse Association. SHTA's primary focus is to unite all Seychelles tourism industry stakeholders under one association in order to be better prepared to defend the interest of the industry and its sustainability as the pillar of the country's economy.

International Coalition of Tourism Partners (ICTP)
Website: www.tourismpartners.org

ICTP is a travel and tourism coalition of global destinations committed to Quality Services and Green Growth.

International Institute for Peace through Tourism
Website: www.iipt.org

IIPT is dedicated to fostering tourism initiatives that contribute to international understanding and cooperation.

ITB Asia 2017
Website: www.itb-asia.com
25 to 27 October 2017 Marina Bay Sands®, Singapore.
ITB Asia is the leading B2B travel trade event for the entire Asia-Pacific region.

Tourism, Hotel Investment and Networking Conference 2017
Website: www.thincafrica..com
THINC Africa 2017 takes place in Cape Town, South Africa from 6-7 September.

The Hotel Show Africa 2017
Website: TheHotelShowAfrica.com
Thousands of hospitality professionals from around the world will be at Gallagher Convention Centre in Johannesburg from 25-27 June.

The Safari Awards
Website: www.safariawards.com
Safari Award finalists are amongst the top 3% in Africa and the winners are unquestionably the best.

PAHTC 2017
Website: www.panafricanhealthtourismcongress.com
08-09 June 2017 at the City of uMhlathuze in KwaZulu-Natal, South Africa.
The Pan-African Health Tourism Congress is being staged to address the interests and needs of Health Tourism Stakeholders in Africa.

List on Africa's dedicated booking portal

Accommodation
Adventure
Activities
Events
Tours

Bookings2Africa.com
Bringing Africa to the World and the World to Africa

📞 +27 (0)72 224 9971 🏠 www.bookings2africa.com ✉ bev@bookings2africa.com

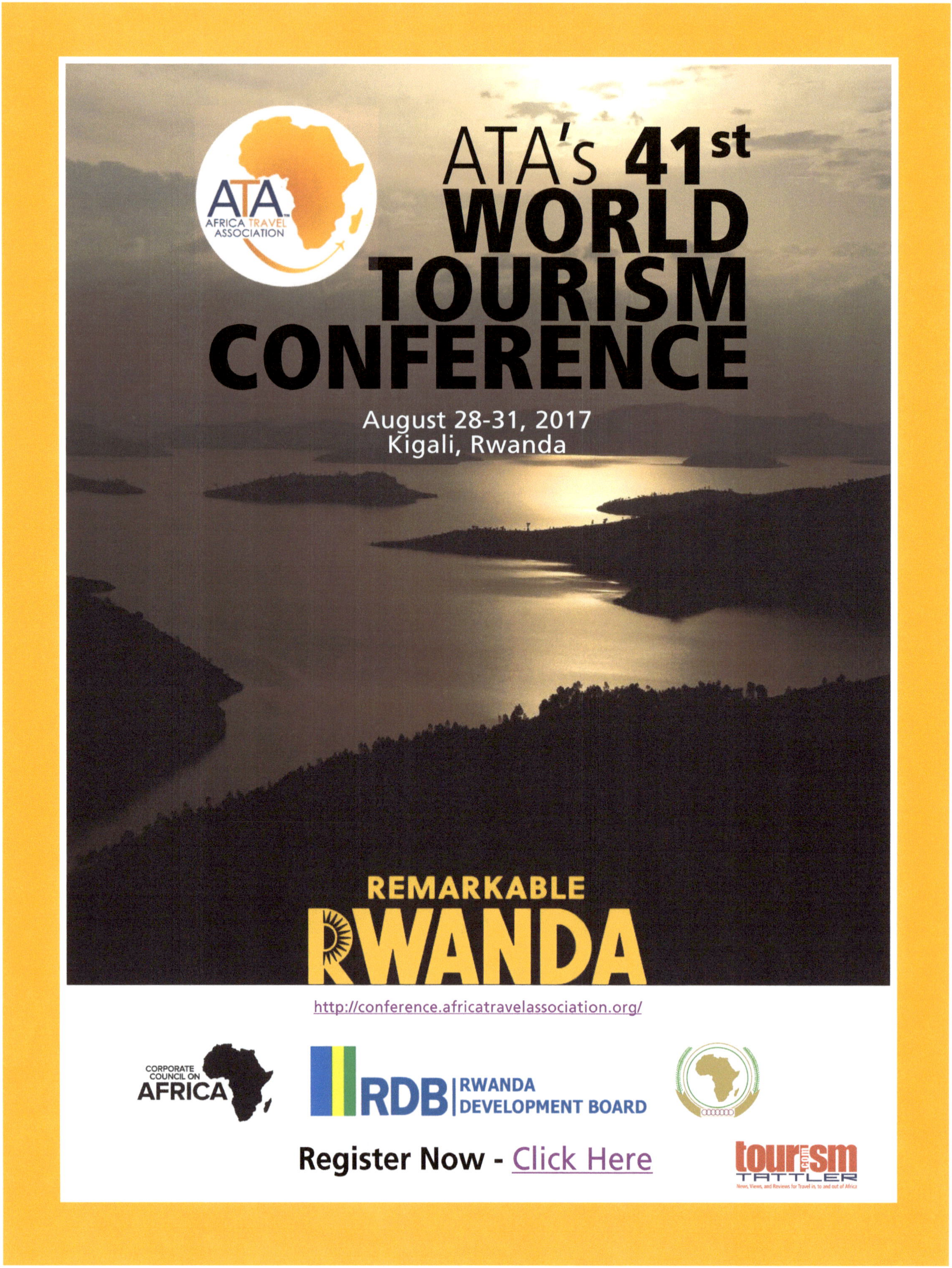

ASSOCIATION EVENT MEDIA PARTNER

ATA's 41st WORLD TOURISM CONFERENCE

August 28-31, 2017
Kigali, Rwanda

REMARKABLE RWANDA

http://conference.africatravelassociation.org/

Register Now - Click Here

SUSTAINABLE TOURISM SOLUTIONS

Conscious Conferencing

Spier Wine Farm (outside Stellenbosch) has implemented numerous initiatives to reduce the carbon footprint of their conferencing facilities, from careful recycling and consistently making sure the area is waste-free, to water conservation technology and training staff in the ways of being eco-friendly.

There's a surge in international travellers looking for sustainable hotels, conference centres, tour experiences and wedding options, tracking down accommodation that has the highest green credentials.

Business travellers are also increasingly mindful of the impact their travel has on our environment. With a strong sense of contributing to saving the planet, they are calling for conference organisers to up their game.

Realising that conference organisers need to quickly locate facilities for green meetings, Spier has implemented a number of initiatives to reduce its carbon footprint; from careful recycling and consistently making sure the area is waste-free, to water conservation technology and training staff in the ways of being eco-friendly. Here are a few eco-friendly tips from Spier's conferencing team:

Adding Meaning to Conference Bookings

Spier has partnered with [Pack for Purpose](), an international project that impacts communities around the world by assisting travellers who want to bring meaningful contributions to destinations.

Spier has selected three projects (an old age home, a community library and primary school) where guests can donate much-needed items.

Environmental Commitment

Spier is committed to reducing its environmental footprint. Over the past decade, municipal water usage has been reduced by 50% and energy by 30%.

There are over 400 water-saving devices on showers, basins and toilets at Spier. Natural light and ventilation and energy-efficient lighting is used where possible. 100% of organic waste and wastewater as well as more than 98% of solid waste are recycled.

A rigorous monitoring and measurement system means that conference organisers can measure the footprint of each delegate. Conference packs are great opportunities to communicate the sustainability story to delegates. One could include a solar lamp or indigenous plant as a gift (these can be obtained from the Tree-preneurs nursery which offers plants nurtured by its network of growers).

On the table, Spier places pens and notebooks of 100% recycled paper for delegate's use. Leftover stationery can be donated to schoolchildren from surrounding communities. Instead of plastic bottled water, Spier offers filtered bottled water which is served in reusable glass bottles.

At Breaktime

During break times, snacks are selected that are healthy both for the planet and body. Spier offers a variety of teas and organic rooibos as well as filter coffee from Avanti, a roastery that supports sustainable coffee farming and fair trade practices. In addition to healthy locally sourced nuts and dried fruit snacks, Spier also offers freshly baked biscuits from the Khayelitsha Cookie Company – a social upliftment project which hires previously unemployed women from that providing skills, training and permanent employment.

Cuisine Choices

Spier offers sustainable conference food that is made with seasonal locally sourced and ethically reared ingredients. Cuisine dishes are made with ingredients that are sourced from the farm, or nearby trusted suppliers who share Spier's sustainable ethos. Fresh produce in Spier's food gardens is grown without the use of pesticides and artificial fertilisers. Eggs are laid by hens that roam freely in Spier's pastures. To prevent overfishing, Spier only serve fish that are listed "green" by the South African Sustainable Seafood Initiative.

Inspiring Excursions

Spier offers excursions that can inspire delegates to make a positive difference. A number of activities are offered that showcase its sustainability efforts – delegates can visit the environmentally friendly wastewater treatment plant, or take a tour of the Tree-preneurs nursery. They can also collect eggs from the free-roaming chickens and also learn about organic gardening in the food garden.

Join Fair Trade To Move Toward Sustainability

Fair Trade Tourism (FTT) launched a new membership programme in May aimed at tourism businesses that need support for their sustainability measures but do not have the resources to become certified in the short term.

For an annual membership fee, ranging from 1,100 (ZAR) for a sole enterprise to 6,000 (ZAR) for a business with 26-50 staff members, Fair Trade Tourism will guide businesses along the sustainability path, focusing on areas such as legal compliance, labour and staff management, reducing energy, water and waste, fair purchasing and improving market access.

Commenting on the entry level programme, Jane Edge, Managing Director of FTT said: "Our aim is to bring smaller businesses into the Fair Trade Tourism value chain, to encourage them to operate more sustainably and to expose them to tour operators who support sustainable efforts. By lowering the threshold for enterprises to access our business development services, we hope to broaden our sustainability impact and contribute to more inclusive growth of the tourism industry."

Aspirant members need to be approved by FTT's Client Advisory Committee and to sign a pledge committing them to year-on-year improvements in their sustainability measures. Applicants fill out a self-evaluation form online about their sustainability actions and FTT will produce a gap analysis highlighting areas where the business needs to improve. FTT will provide the toolkits, templates, and advice required to assist businesses along the sustainability path.

For more information, contact Thiofhi Ravele, Business Development Services Manager at *thiofhi@fairtrade.travel* or apply online on at *www.fairtrade.travel*.

Fair Trade Tourism has partnered with Tourism Tattler in supporting the aims and aspirations of the
2017 International Year of Sustainable Tourism for Development.
Through a series of editorial features published throughout this year, Tourism Tattler will be profiling a selection of Fair Trade certified tourism businesses who meet and in many cases exceed, sustainable tourism practices.

View Fair Trade's Sustainable Tourism Gems already listed on the
UNWTO #IYSTD2017 official website at:
www.tourism4development2017.org

+27 (0)12 342 2945
www.fairtrade.travel

PARTNER   SPECIAL FEATURE   AFRICA'S SUSTAINABLE TOURISM GEMS

HOME SEARCH ○ ABOUT ○ GET INVOLVED ○ BLOG ○ CONTACT US | GET LISTED ON ECO ATLAS ✓

Launching Africa's sustainable tourism gems this month with a selection of South Africa's eco-friendly hotels and lodges, Tourism Tattler has partnered with Eco Atlas – an award winning eco-travel choice website. Where a featured eco-friendly property is already listed on Eco Atlas, we've shown the applicable icons.

RESOURCE USE

 **Water Saving:** 3 or more of the following practices in place: a no-leak policy, water audit, flow restrictors on taps and shower heads, dual flush toilet cisterns, harvesting rain water, utilising waste water (grey water), only watering early morning and evening, alien tree removal, planting water wise, drip irrigation system, compost toilet, garden well mulched.

 **Energy Saving**: 3 or more of the following practices in place: energy A- rated appliances, low energy bulbs, geezer blankets and/or timers, established electricity strategy such as switching off appliances and lights when not being used.

 **Recycling:** Established policy to reduce and re-use waste, the recycling of any of the following resources: Paper, Glass, Tin, Plastic and Organic Matter, on-site composting and wormeries.

 **Renewable Energy**: Utilising solar and/or wind energy through solar panels and/or wind turbines.

 **Green Design:** Incorporated into the design of the building: proper insulation, sustainable and renewable building materials, maximising light and energy from the sun, building with recycled materials, non-toxic paints and other building materials, water and energy efficiency.

 **Carbon Neutral:** Planting of trees to off-set the carbon footprint of the establishment and its guests.

EARTH FRIENDLY

 **Eco Cleaning Agents:** utilising or selling products that are fully biodegradable, free of harmful chemicals and not tested on animals.

 **Eco Body Products:** Utilising or selling body products that are fully biodegradable, free of harmful chemicals and not tested on animals.

 **Eco Packaging:** Utilising or selling fully biodegradable packaging and take-away containers made from renewable resources. Accepting returns on product packaging for re-use.

PEOPLE AND EARTH

 **Biodiversity:** no use of pesticides or poisons, planting only indigenous, conservation of indigenous flora and fauna on your property, alien vegetation removal and rehabilitation of indigenous.

 **Local Products:** utilising products grown or manufactured within a 100km radius, the producing or selling of local products.

 **Organic Food:** Utilising or selling food that is produced using a system that sustains the health of soils, ecosystems and people without the use of inputs with adverse effects for biodiversity.

 **Fair Trade:** selling products or implementing policies which contribute to sustainable development by offering better trading conditions to, and securing the rights of, marginalized producers and workers. Registered with Fair Trade Tourism or Fair Trade Label SA.

 **Empowerment:** Skills development, training and profit share programmes which empower staff and enable better working conditions and work opportunities.

ANIMAL FRIENDLY

 **Free Range Chicken:** raised in a humane manner with freedom to roam and constant access to vegetation, fresh air and fresh water. Chickens free of hormones and antibiotics (check with your supplier if they meet all these requirements)

 **Free Range Eggs:** chickens raised in a humane manner with freedom to roam and constant access to vegetation, fresh air and fresh water. Chickens free of hormones and antibiotics (check with your supplier if they meet all these requirements)

 **Badger Friendly Honey**: utilising or selling honey accredited with the Endangered Wildlife Trust certificate to ensure no honey badgers are harmed in the production of the honey.

 **Ethically Farmed Products:** utilising or selling free range meat and/or wool products that are have wildlife friendly management strategies which do not include the trapping, hunting, poisoning and killing of predators. Fair Game endorsed products.

 **Sustainable Fishing:** utilising, promoting or selling sustainable seafood from well managed fisheries as listed in the South African Sustainable Seafood Initiative (SASSI).

 **Free Range Pork**: Raised in a humane manner with freedom to roam outdoors and constant access to vegetation, fresh air and fresh water. Pigs free of hormones and antibiotics and their feed free of animal by-products (check with your supplier if they meet all these requirements)

 **Veg Or Vegan:** Serving purely vegetarian or vegan food, thereby providing healthy eating alternatives and decreasing the amount of natural resources used in the production of food.

AFRICA'S SUSTAINABLE TOURISM GEMS — SPECIAL FEATURE — SOUTH AFRICA

ECO-FRIENDLY HOTELS & LODGES & ATTRACTIONS

Parker Cottage

Parker Cottage in the heart of Cape Town's City Bowl is more than just another bed-and-breakfast hospitality establishment set in a heritage (circa 1895) building. It's arguably the greenest heritage building in the city, and the country for that matter. The new owner, Pamela Nayler aims to prove that not only new build properties can be sustainably run.

And Pamela's aim is being remarkably well achieved, as Parker Cottage's recent Fair Trade Tourism accreditation testifies. Sustainable tourism practices include using rainwater for washing machines and irrigation of their indigenous gardens; water for showers, baths and rooms is heated using energy efficient air source heat pumps; and they actively separate waste for recycling by the needy through The Salvation Army.

In addition, Parker Cottage look after their staff incredibly well. Permanent staff receive 50% higher wages than the minimum prescribed benchmark for the industry and are motivated with guaranteed Christmas bonuses and inflation beating annual pay increases. Staff are also funded for at least one training course a year to ensure that they are up skilled and advanced on their career path.

Their commitment to community engagement and support includes anonymous funding of two school scholarships at St Pauls Primary in the Bo Kaap, regular donations of old linen, towelling, crockery, bedding and soaps to The Haven Nightshelter, supporting the work of Medicins Sans Frontiers with monthly donations, and sponsoring at least three room nights a year to charity organisations around Cape Town for raffles or other fundraising efforts.

Economic development projects include a policy to purchase supplies and services from businesses located in less affluent areas and owned by historically disadvantaged families and individuals. One such individual is their driver and guide, Chris Hannival, who was encouraged and supported to start his own transport business. Chris now offers work to a further two drivers as a result.

Travel. Enjoy. Respect. #IYSTD17

QUICK LINKS:

📞 +27(0)21 424 6445   ✉ info@parkercottage.co.za   🏠 www.parkercottage.co.za

f @ParkerCottageGuesthouse   ▶ Parker Cottage

SOUTH AFRICA   AFRICA'S SUSTAINABLE TOURISM GEMS

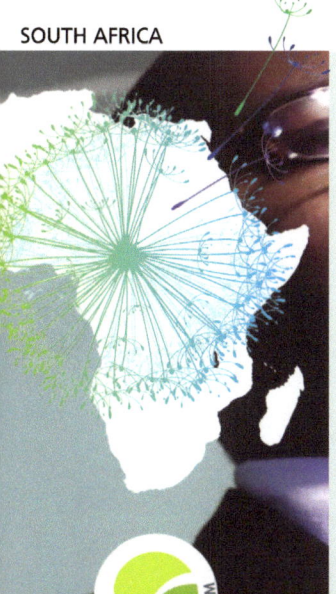

Coffeebeans Routes

Travel is about sharing experiences and few tour operators enable guests to immerse themselves in South Africa's extraordinary mix of culture and creativity better than Coffeebeans Routes.

Established in 2005, Coffeebeans has created a formidable reputation as a cultural and creative tour operator, by focusing on stories. As founder and creative director Iain Harris puts it: *"We build experiences around stories because everybody has them. In South Africa, where most of the population was legislated into silence, our stories can be equalisers. And this is African tourism's great opportunity."*

Coffeebeans Routes prioritises creativity. They create travel experiences around South African stories – contemporary, urban, African experiences that provide nuanced insights and complexity. They offer experiences in Cape Town and Johannesburg, working with a network of locals, from tourist guides, cooks, musicians, fashion designers and artists, to architects, spiritual leaders, brewers, wine-makers, historians, and everything in between.

Using tourism as a key to unlock economic potential, Coffeebeans enables visitors to explore the country's cultural diversity and legacy, and they manage it by creating sustainable development. Their approach to sustainable tourism practice is to focus on social justice, while in parallel implementing tangible sustainable tourism projects.

Says Iain: *"Environmental impact starts with social justice. If radical social and economic disparities are reduced, if society becomes more equal, environmental sustainability is a natural byproduct. So the starting point for us is social justice, and our biggest impact is through a responsible approach to how we engage with people, communities and stories, and how positioning new narratives at the heart of tourism starts to level imbalances. When we start to take ownership of the environments we live in (given that so much has been taken away, making us indentured tenants rather than curators), we naturally minimise impact on the natural environment."*

Coffeebeans Routes story telling tours have become so successful that they have been the recipient of many award accolades, including the African Responsible Tourism Awards.

Travel. Enjoy. Respect. #IYSTD17

QUICK LINKS:

📞 +27 (0)21 813 9829   ✉ info@coffeebeansroutes.com   🏠 www.coffeebeansroutes.com

f @coffeebeansroutes   🐦 @coffeebeansrout   g+ Coffeebeans Routes   ▶ Coffeebeans Routes

SOUTH AFRICA — SPECIAL FEATURE — AFRICA'S SUSTAINABLE TOURISM GEMS

ECO-FRIENDLY HOTELS & LODGES & ATTRACTIONS

SPIER: COMMITTED TO SUSTAINABLE TOURISM

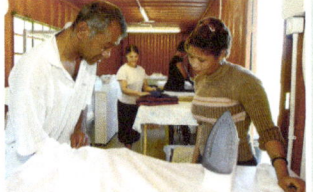

As one of South Africa's oldest wine farms and a well-known Western Cape landmark, Spier is passionate about the environment and supporting the local community. It regularly buys from and supports trusted local suppliers, and its philosophy is to make a difference every day in the lives of its guests, staff, the environment, and community.

A sustainability pioneer over the past 15 years, Spier today recycles 100% of its wastewater and over 98% of its solid waste. It is a WWF Conservation Champion and is accredited by Fair Trade Tourism and the Wine Industry Ethical Trade Association. Its cellar carries FSSC 22000 certification and Fairtrade accreditation.

Three centuries since Spier's start in 1692, the farm is still family-owned. The Enthoven family bought it in 1993, lives on the farm and works with the Spier team to bring positive change to the environment and community. Today Spier has a fresh, conscious energy, and is focused on art and good, ethical farming. It produces six ranges of award-winning wines and serves seasonal farm-to-table food at its four-star hotel and three restaurants. Spier's Sustainable Conferencing Toolkit offers conference delegates wanting to do business in an inspiring environment, 12 different meeting venues with varying capacities and settings, as well as various picnic spots and open-air cocktail or dining spaces. Venues include the four-star, 153-room Spier Hotel with boardroom; 400-seater auditorium; historic Manor House and adjacent oak-shaded courtyard; and three river- and mountain-facing conference rooms which can be combined to seat 150 delegates in school room style.

QUICK LINKS:

- +27 (0)42 203 1111
- info@spier.co.za
- www.spier.co.za
- @SpierWineFarm
- @spierwinefarm
- Spier Wine Farm
- spierwinefarm
- Spier Hotel

BUSINESS & FINANCE

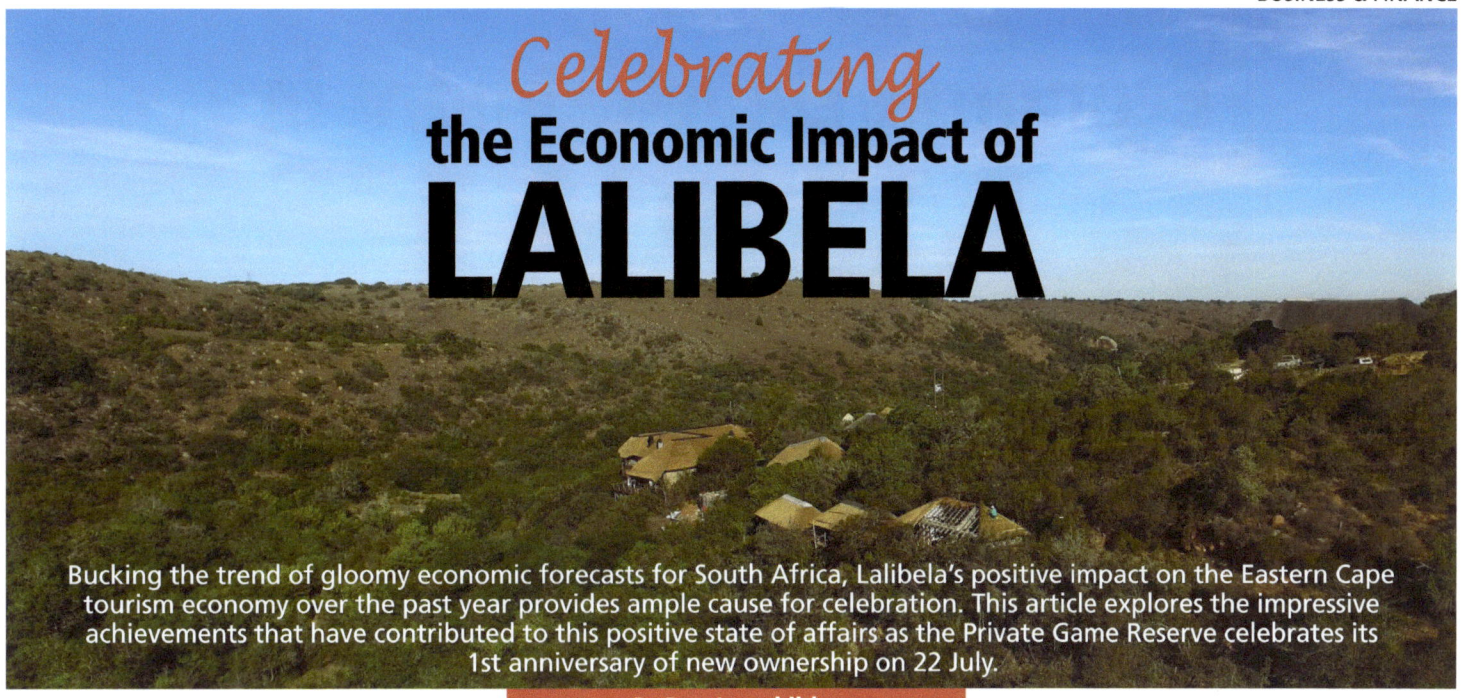

Celebrating the Economic Impact of LALIBELA

Bucking the trend of gloomy economic forecasts for South Africa, Lalibela's positive impact on the Eastern Cape tourism economy over the past year provides ample cause for celebration. This article explores the impressive achievements that have contributed to this positive state of affairs as the Private Game Reserve celebrates its 1st anniversary of new ownership on 22 July.

By **Des Langkilde**.

Heralding a New Era in Private Sector Conservation

The sale of Lalibela and the subsequent purchase of an additional 4,000 hectares of adjacent land, is seen as a major vote of confidence for the Eastern Cape game lodge industry as a whole. The reserve now stretches over 10,444h (approximately 25,700 acres), with the Big-5 area being some 7,500h combined with the adjacent breeding area of 2,900h. In addition to the fiscal boost that this investment has had on the province, the erection of over 39km of new game fencing has contributed to local employment.

Environmental Rehabilitation. Adding to local employment, approximately R400,000 a month has been spent on the removal of alien vegetation like black wattle and prickly pear. So far, about 280h of wattle forest has been cleared and transformed into savannah grassland. In addition, approximately 225h of alien invasive prickly pear has been removed. This represents a significant commitment to preserving South Africa's natural heritage, and of course to the enhancement of overall guest experiences for visitors.

Game Repopulation. In keeping with Lalibela's conservation vision to keep the indigenous flora and fauna in equilibrium, Lalibela has embarked on a major game repopulation drive. Significant game numbers have already been purchased, primarily from within the province, and have been placed in the Big-5 area as well as the breeding areas. Species include buffalo, zebra, black wildebeest, giraffe, kudu, impala, eland and waterbuck. These will augment the already impressive density of game at Lalibela as well as form the nuclei of core breeding herds.

Game Monitoring. Contraception of certain species like elephant and lion has been carried out. This is in keeping with the game carrying capacity of the reserve, which formed part of a report by a team of game management experts commissioned to analyse the ideal ratio of herbivores to predators that the reserve can sustain, based on the five biomes found here.

Anti-Poaching. Where previously, Rangers performed anti-poaching duties, Lalibela now has a dedicated anti-poaching team that operates 24-hours a day, 365 days a year. They are equipped with the latest telemetry and night vision equipment and are able to protect the reserves growing list of endangered species.

Lodge Upgrades. Soft refurbishments have taken place at Tree Tops and Mark's Camp and a major refurb is almost complete at Lentaba Lodge. In addition, two new rooms are being added to Lentaba, which increases the total room count to 10 – 5 classic rooms and 5 luxury rooms.

Technology Upgrades. Lalibela has significantly upgraded the WiFi service bandwidth so that guests' devices automatically connect as soon as they arrive at their lodge.

New Private Villa. Hillside Private Villa, a historic 100-year old farmhouse positioned on an elevated site with sweeping views over the expansive valley below and its own water hole, is in the process of being renovated. This exclusive use home-style villa offers 5 double or twin bedrooms to accommodate a maximum of 10 guests and is due to launch in September 2017.

Ranger Training. Funding has been made available for all Lalibela's game rangers to further their qualifications. In addition to attaining their next level up in Field Guiding, some of the Rangers have completed electives, with 3 rangers having achieved excellent results on a recent tracking and track interpretation exam.

New Staff Housing. Lalibela's commitment to staff welfare includes an investment of R4m to upgrade the standard of staff accommodation. The staff are about to move into their new modern abode, where each unit has hot and cold running water, electricity, a lounge, kitchen, and indoor toilet. The units have been positioned to provide a sense of community with a paved courtyard where staff can socialise with family and friends. In addition, new management housing has been built, while various old buildings such as farm houses, old staff housing and unsightly sheds have been destroyed and removed from sight.

New Water Supply. Lalibela has two huge freshwater dams on the newly bought property (which forms part of the breeding area). This clear, drinking quality water is pumped up to a new 150,000-litre holding reservoir and from there, it is gravity fed to the lodges and staff housing.

Water Recycling. The new sewerage and waste water treatment plant, built to convert grey water from all the lodges and staff housing into clear drinking water, is also used to fill numerous water holes on the reserve.

Overall, Lalibela's positive impact on the economy of the Eastern Cape in just one year of operating under new ownership and management is laudable. On behalf of the travel trade, we salute you!

For more information visit www.lalibela.net

BUSINESS & FINANCE

Economic Development in AFRICA

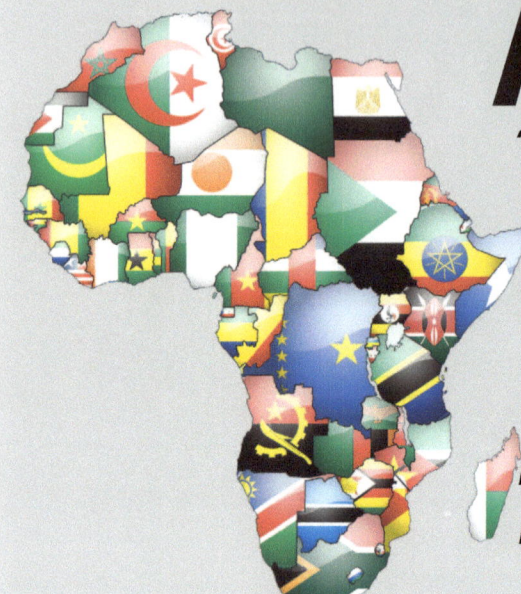

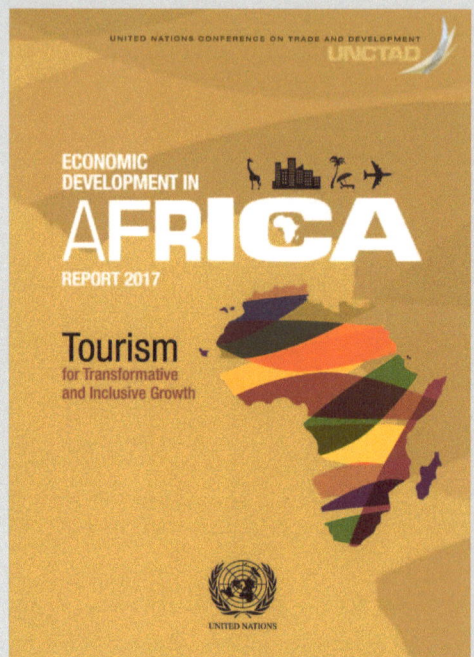

"Africa is in the best ever position as a global tourism player. Most African countries, even where tourism is the main economic activity, lack strategically integrated product development and regional tourism policies.

This report helps address these issues. Going forward, African tourism needs to be grounded in sound interregional and intraregional policies, and should promote strong intersectoral linkages. Tourism in isolation will struggle to prosper."

Carmen Nibigira, Regional Coordinator, East Africa Tourism Platform

Following the United Nations Conference on Trade and Development (UNCTAD) held in Geneva, Switzerland in January 2017, an in-depth report has been published on tourism for transformative and Inclusive growth in Africa. Here are a few of the startling findings contained in the report.

The Economic Development in Africa Report 2017: Tourism for Transformative and Inclusive Growth examines the role that tourism can play in Africa's development process. It argues that tourism can be an engine for inclusive growth and economic development and that it can complement development strategies aimed at fostering economic diversification and structural transformation within the right policy context.

The report does not focus on climate change or its financing aspects as these have been taken up in much greater detail in recent publications on the sector. The focus is rather on enhancing the role that tourism can play in socioeconomic development, poverty alleviation, trade, fostering regional integration and structural transformation. To achieve all of this, Africa must tackle key impediments to developing the tourism sector, such as weak intersectoral linkages.

Since the United Nations designated 2017 as the International Year of Sustainable Tourism for Development, the tourism sector has been praised for its capacity to stimulate economic growth through the creation of jobs and by attracting investment and fostering entrepreneurship, while also contributing, if properly harnessed, to preservation of ecosystems and biodiversity, protection of cultural heritage and promotion of empowerment of local communities.

Tourism can be an engine for inclusive growth and sustainable economic development. Since the 1990s, tourism has increasingly contributed to Africa's growth, employment and trade. During 1995–2014, international tourist arrivals to Africa grew by an average of 6 per cent per year and tourism export revenues, 9 per cent per year. The average total contribution of tourism to gross domestic product (GDP) increased from $69 billion in 1995–1998 to $166 billion in 2011–2014, that is from 6.8 per cent of GDP in Africa to 8.5 per cent of GDP. Furthermore, tourism generated more than 21 million jobs on average in 2011–2014, which translates into 7.1 per cent of all jobs in Africa. This means that over the period 2011–2014, the tourism industry was supporting 1 out of every 14 jobs. At the same time, tourism has also been associated with operating in isolation from other parts of the economy, suffering from high financial leakage, generating sociocultural tensions and environmental damage. History suggests that countries cannot rely on tourism as the sole avenue out of poverty or the only pathway to sustainable economic development.

Tourism's potential has been recognized by policymakers at the national and international levels, and is increasingly reflected in national and international policy frameworks. At the global level, Sustainable Development Goals 8, 12 and 14 highlight the central role of tourism in job creation, local promotion of culture and economic development. However, as tourism covers several sectors and is a cross-cutting issue, the development of tourism has an impact on many Sustainable Development Goals, for example poverty, decent work, gender and infrastructure development.

Some of the key questions addressed in the report include:
- How does tourism contribute to structural transformation and more inclusive growth?
- How can linkages between tourism and other productive sectors be harnessed to create additional economic opportunities and provide sustainable livelihoods?
- How can the economic potential of intraregional tourism be fostered and better exploited through deeper regional integration?
- What is the relationship between tourism and peace?

BUSINESS & FINANCE

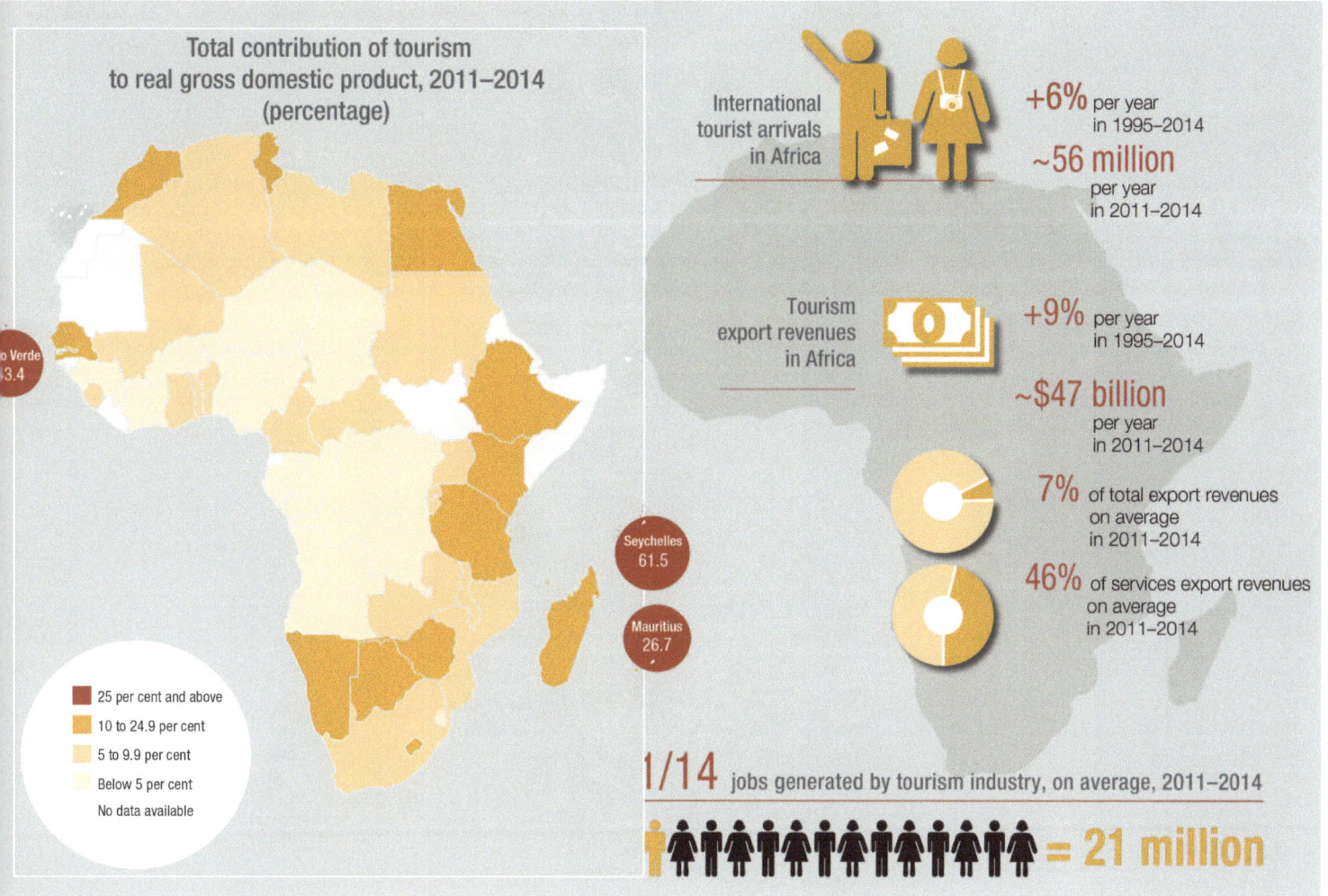

The main findings are as follows:

First, tourism can promote economic diversification and structural transformation in Africa, with linkages between tourism and other productive sectors playing a fundamental role in this regard. To unlock the potential of intersectoral linkages to contribute to structural transformation, cross-sectoral issues need to be aligned with, and integrated into, policy frameworks at the national, regional and continental levels.

Second, tourism is critical to the continent's inclusive growth and can play an important role in the global fight to reduce poverty and achieve the Sustainable Development Goals. Beyond generating economic benefits and boosting productive capacities, tourism has the potential to foster inclusion by creating employment opportunities among vulnerable groups such as the poor, women and youth.

Third, continental and intraregional tourism in Africa is increasing and offers opportunities for economic and export diversification if its potential is exploited at the national and regional levels. African countries would benefit if they made further progress with the free movement of persons, currency convertibility and liberalizing air transport services. This would facilitate greater access to tourism destinations and boost the competitiveness of destinations. It also requires regional economic communities and countries to comprehensively plan for intraregional and continental tourism.

Fourth, peace is essential for tourism, and the development of tourism can foster peace. African countries with tourism potential should implement policies that strengthen the sector as these policies will contribute to both peace and development. The analysis and findings of the report also confirm the bidirectional causal relationship between peace and tourism and further show that the effect of peace on tourism is much greater in magnitude than the impact of tourism on peace.

And finally, Chapter 6 of the report recapitulates some of the main findings, key messages and policy recommendations. The chapter concludes that there is an urgent need to address the lack of tourism data and suggests that this could be undertaken as part of ongoing efforts to improve macroeconomic data collection.

African Governments, in collaboration with development partners, need to develop and implement effective methods of collecting tourism data to accurately assess the sector's contribution to social and economic development. However, at present, many countries are experiencing a severe shortage of basic tourism statistics. There is little information on how different components of the tourism sector contribute to its aggregate impact, the distribution of such impacts or how they may be increased. Considering the large amount of data required for evaluating supply- and demand-related aggregates, it remains a challenge to effectively disaggregate available data to evaluate how economic impact varies by type of tourist, type of tourism or the structure of the sector. There is a dearth of available data on tourism activities categorized by gender and an inconsistent measurement of flows of cross-border traders (a sub-category of business tourists) on the continent. In part, accurate measurement of the effects of tourism policy analysis is also hindered because the sector is not designated as an industry in standard economic accounts. This highlights the need of government for improved data, for enhanced quantitative and economic policy analysis of the sector.

The full Report can be downloaded as a PDF file HERE.

BUSINESS & FINANCE

Market Intelligence Report

SATSA – Southern Africa Tourism Services Association

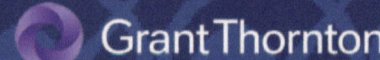

The information below was extracted from data available as at **07 July 2017**. By Martin Jansen van Vuuren of Grant Thornton.

ARRIVALS

The latest available data from Statistics South Africa is for **January to April 2017***:

	Current period	Change over same period last year
UK	187 569	2.9%
Germany	138 976	15.9%
USA	107 882	7.2%
India	28 340	2.8%
China (incl Hong Kong)	36 630	-12.0%
Overseas Arrivals	972 671	11.3%
African Arrivals	2 564 797	-2.8%
Total Foreign Arrivals	3 541 299	0.7%

HOTEL STATS

The latest available data from STR Global is for **January to May 2017**:

Current period	Average Room Occupancy (ARO)	Average Room Rate (ARR)	Revenue Per Available Room (RevPAR)
All Hotels in SA	64.2%	R 1 269	R 815
All 5-star hotels in SA	66.8%	R 2 360	R 1 576
All 4-star hotels in SA	65.7%	R 1 172	R 771
All 3-star hotels in SA	63.3%	R 946	R 599
Change over same period last year			
All Hotels in SA	-0.8%	5.9%	5.1%
All 5-star hotels in SA	-1.3%	6.0%	4.7%
All 4-star hotels in SA	1.2%	6.2%	7.5%
All 3-star hotels in SA	0.2%	3.3%	3.5%

ACSA DATA

The latest available data from ACSA is for **January to May 2017**:

Change over same period last year	Passengers arriving on International Flights	Passengers arriving on Regional Flights	Passengers arriving on Domestic Flights
OR Tambo International	3.7%	-1.3%	0.6%
Cape Town International	26.3%	3.4%	2.6%
King Shaka International	11.6%	N/A	4.9%

CAR RENTAL DATA

The latest available data from SAVRALA is for **January to December 2016**:

	Current period	Change over same period last year
Industry Rental Days	16 936 276	7%
Industry Utilisation	71.6%	1.5%
Industry Revenue	5 294 680 207	12%

WHAT THIS MEANS FOR MY BUSINESS

The data indicates a slow down in the domestic market. Growth in passengers arriving on domestic flights are subdued across all three airports monitored and the growth in occupancies and average room rate for 3-star hotels (who have proportionally more domestic guests than 5-star hotels) are low.

*Note that African Arrivals plus Overseas Arrivals do not add to Total Foreign Arrivals due to the exclusion of unspecified arrivals, which could not be allocated to either African or Overseas.

For more information contact Martin at Grant Thornton on +27 (0)21 417 8838 or visit: http://www.gt.co.za

BUSINESS & FINANCE

Hotel Valuation Index Africa

The third edition of the HVS/STR African Hotel Valuation Index offers critical information on 21 African hotel markets and the countries, including hotel value changes and projections through 2016 and intelligence on market dynamics.

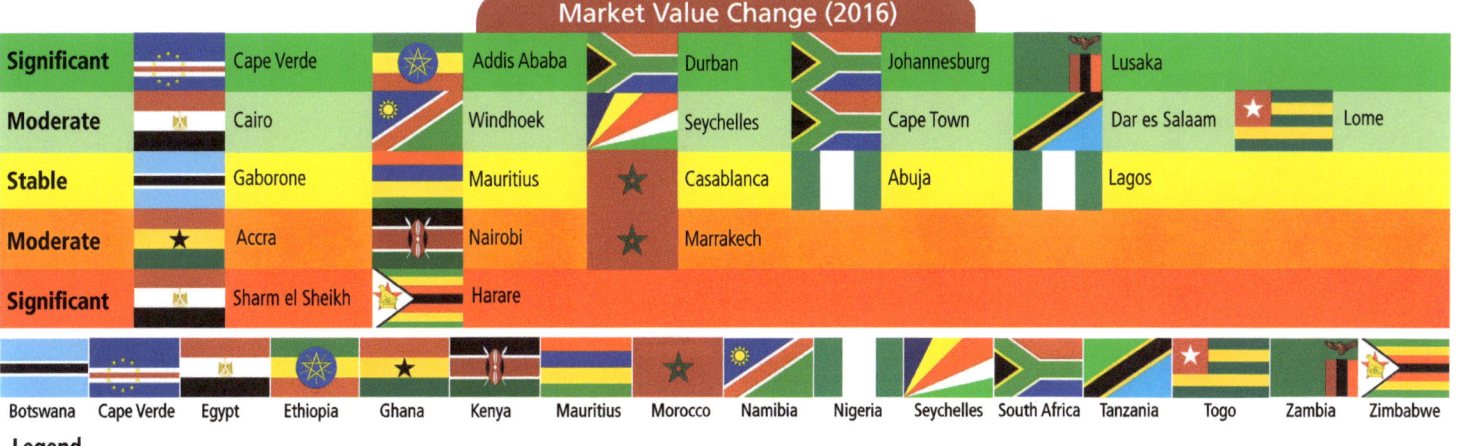

Note: Numerous factors influence the value of an individual asset, including the property's age, condition, location, amenities and services, brand, management expertise, and reputation. These factors must all be considered in the context of the hotel's specific competitive market, including the nature, strength, and trends in demand generators; the character and competitive posture of the existing hotels; and the potential addition of any new properties. The value of any individual asset can only be concluded after a thorough investigation of all these factors. And that conclusion will invariably differ—often materially—from the index indicated by the HVI. Although the HVI cannot tell you what a particular hotel is worth, it does provide excellent "big picture" data, indicating which market areas are experiencing positive trends for investment opportunities.

HVS Africa Market Summary by Country

Botswana - Gabarone

Botswana is one of Africa's success stories. Real GDP growth has been around 5% per annum over the past 10 years. After suffering negative growth in 2015, mainly due to the downturn in China and falling commodities prices, the economy grew around 3.7% in 2016.

The Botswana hospitality industry is one sector of the economy continuing to thrive. Marriott announced a new 160 bedroom Protea hotel in the Gaborone CBD. Cresta Hotels is opening the 83 bedroom Cresta Maun resort in 2017. Much of the economic success is a result of sound macro-economic policies; resulting in the World Bank describing Botswana as "a development success story".

This strong endorsement is assisting the overall demand for hotels for business travelers in Gaborone. In addition Botswana is lucky enough to have two of the outstanding tourist destinations on the continent, Chobe National Park and the Okavango Delta, thus drawing significant numbers of leisure travelers to the country. Combined, business and leisure travelers have resulting in occupancy of 65-70% over the past few years. Such stable performance, despite a growth in ADR (in local currency) demonstrates the health of the market.

An improvement in global economies is crucial to further growth in the Gaborone hotel market; higher demand and prices for commodities and diamonds will lead to increased corporate demand, whilst improved economic confidence at home will encourage more tourists to the country.

Botswana enjoys political stability and strong economic recovery that will benefit the Gaborone hotel market. Investors are showing interest again and Hilton has announced the opening of its first property in the capital, proving its confidence in the market's potential to grow. In 2016, both occupancy and ADR picked up, boosting the values up by 6.1%.

For detailed analysis visit http://hvi.hvs.com/market/africa/Botswana_-_Gaborone

BUSINESS & FINANCE

HVS Africa Market Summary by Country

Cape Verde

Cape Verde's economy is an exemplary example of a stable political environment and a working democracy. A steady economic growth path has been followed by a rising quality of life for its citizens. This is all despite the country not having an abundance of natural resources, occasional drought and a small agricultural base. Given this success and the ability of the islands to attract European guests for leisure breaks, HVS felt it was an interesting market to include in the HVI.

Tourism is one of the main contributors to the economy of Cape Verde. Foreign direct investment is active in the country due to high levels of investor confidence arising from a stable political and economic environment and a growing market. The country attracts tourists from Europe, in particular the United Kingdom, Germany and Portugal due to strong national and cultural ties

The hotel industry is a beneficiary of the FDI that the country enjoys. A new Resort Group property was constructed on Sal Island and launched in November 2016. Thereafter they have plans for several other hotels in the main islands, all of which will be branded by international hoteliers.

The market is evolving rapidly and as such neither occupancy nor ADR can be seen as stable, yet. However, as both the number of visitors to the islands and hotel supply continue to increase the future for the hotel industry looks positive.

Cape Verde is growing into a mature market, with a stabilized strong occupancy and profitable rate levels. The Resort Group built a strong business model to enhance tourism growth, while adding more rooms to the market. Additional flights to the islands have been confirmed and this should push the occupancy up at a steady pace. Occupancy will surpass the 75% threshold and rates are expected to grow by 5%, pushing REVPAR and values up by 10.7%.

For detailed analysis visit http://hvi.hvs.com/market/africa/Cape_Verde

Egypt

Egypt has had more than its fair share of terror-related incidents. Politically the country still has issues to resolve with marathon court cases against the Muslim Brotherhood featuring prominently in global media. Security concerns are currently exerting a negative impact on the country's tourism outlook.

The economic landscape of Egypt has been a mixed bag. The biggest news was the announcement of a planned $60 billion infrastructure investment by Saudi Arabia. The economy started to recover in 2014/15, as the government scaled up infrastructure spending and undertook important measures to restore macroeconomic stability. As such the World Bank reported, growth rebounded to 4.2% in 2014/15, double the growth during the previous four years.

Cairo

In Cairo, occupancy increased to above 50% whilst ADR remained flat. The performance can be attributed to the return of international visitors to Egypt after the political unrest of late 2013 and early 2014. Travel resulting from Eid al-Adha also aided performance in the market. Hotel values still achieved a respectable 18.6% increase in 2015, although remain below the levels in 2011.

Cairo will experience a slight recovery. The increased demand in corporate guests from the Middle East and Europe will boost the demand up by 6%. The hotels should give priority to occupancy and the ADR will remain stable in real terms. 2016 was a recovery year in Cairo; values shot up to US$78k, the highest figure experienced since 2011.

For detailed analysis visit http://hvi.hvs.com/market/africa/Egypt_-_Cairo

Sharm el Sheikh

Sharm-el-Sheikh has not had the same fortunes as Cairo. Occupancy levels plunged in Sharm El Sheikh following the crash of a Russian civilian aeroplane in early November 2015. A subsequent ban on travel and cancellation of flights to the region from Russia and various European countries severely impacted performance in the Rea Sea destination. Despite challenging trading, values improved slightly, although Sharm remains in last place on the HVI.

Sharm-el-Sheikh's occupancy is significantly impacted by the violent events that happened within 2015/16. The occupancy rate dropped below 50%, leading the values down by 27.3%. However, whilst this massive drop in values did no good for the hotel businesses, it represented an attractive investment opportunity. Investors can buy at a low price and gain from the cash on sale rather than from the pure operation of the hotel.

For detailed analysis visit http://hvi.hvs.com/market/africa/Egypt_-_Sharm_el_Sheikh

HVS Africa Market Summary by Country

Ethiopia - Addis Ababa

With a "double-digit" GDP growth that is now something of an official mantra, Ethiopia has become the fastest growing economy in the continent and is commonly referred to as "the capital of Africa" for its political, diplomatic and commercial significance.

The increasing number of inbound tourists along with the new supply of offices in the market enhances a significant demand for international standard hotels, which remains for the most unsatisfied. In 2015, 1 million travelers could not find accommodation up to their standards in the city and there will be 3 million in 2020 if new hotels are not built, according to Awash International Bank. In addition, the large diplomatic community and the political activity in Addis Ababa will push MICE activity up significantly.

Addis Ababa concentrates 80% of the Ethiopian's hotel supply much of which is outdated and of poor quality. However, the strong economic fundamentals along with the improvement of the infrastructure attract an increasing number of international hotel groups which will account for 46% of the new supply in the next few years.

Occupancy and rates have been steady in recent years. Addis Ababa experienced occupancy regularly up to 80% and the country has the highest room rate in the continent, according to a survey carried out by STR Global in late 2015.

Hotels' values in Addis-Ababa have been consistent over recent years, rising steadily. They were approximately twice the value of the African Average in 2015. Given the existing level of unsatisfied demand, the new supply is not likely to affect the long term occupancy, and the new branded hotel will push the average rate up, positively impacting the RevPAR. Therefore, value should be sustainable.

The substantial amount of rooms coming into Addis Ababa impacted the occupancy and rate levels in the capital in 2016. Whilst the demand grew by 8%, occupancy grew by only 4 points and the average rate barely followed inflation. However, values reached a peak at US$356,000 per room, proving the investors' confidence and the potential of the market to grow significantly.

For detailed analysis visit http://hvi.hvs.com/market/africa/Ethiopia_-_Addis_Ababa

Ghana - Accra

The concentration of Ghana's international tourist arrivals still revolves between the nation's capital city Accra, and the mining and agriculture regional destinations. However, there is growing demand for hotels in Ghana's second and third tier markets, with many players taking note of the massive potential.

Stakeholders such as hotel operators, investors, developers and the government sectors are closely following the new investments 'hot spots' of Ghana. Hotel chains such as Hilton, Moevenpick Hotels & Resorts, IBIS Styles, InterContinental Hotels Group, Marriott International, Golden Tulip, as well as Ghana's domestic hotel groups such as Fiesta Hospitality Group and African Regent have indicated their intentions of strengthening the presence of their economy to mid-scale brands in the market.

Overall, Accra's tourism industry can expect strong long-term potential, bolstered by rising demand for international, domestic and regional travel.

Future additions to the current supply of hotels will continue to exert some pressure on values. With the recent launch of the Kempinski Accra and the Ibis Styles properties values have fallen slightly in US$ terms, although at a slower rate than previous years.

Due to a substantial amount of supply coming into the market, the level of occupancy dropped by 2 points in 2016 and the average rate experienced slow growth below inflationary levels. However, the opening of branded hotels will help increase the average rate. Poor currency performance leads to a 3.4% drop in values, down to US$218,000 which is the weakest year out of the past five years.

For detailed analysis visit http://hvi.hvs.com/market/africa/Ghana_-_Accra

Kenya - Nairobi

Although the prospect of presidential elections in 2017 may have a negative effect on hotels' performance, the visit of the President of the United States, Barack Obama, and his Holiness the Pope led to an increase in interest for the country.

Nairobi's hotel market presents a mixed picture. While non-branded hotels are struggling and the market performance is down (overall REVPAR down by 6.2%), the international hotel groups continue to see Kenya as a lucrative market for expansion. 2016 - 2018 will see a massive increase in supply of branded hotels offering international standards.

Concurrently, Kenya's hotel market offers significant investment opportunities owing to its position of regional hub for leisure tourism, finance, government and commerce. Foreign investment continues to flow into Kenya, the World Travel and Tourism Council forecast a 5.2% growth in capital investment per annum until 2025. The huge increase of new supply results in a fall in RevPAR. As a result, hotels' values in Nairobi were down 4.8% in 2015. Room supply continues to be a challenge and local demand in Nairobi is now as important as international. As a result, rooms demand is weaker, and that has a negative impact on the overall hotels' profitability. Increased confidence from international travelers along with the growing supply of international brands should boost hotels' performance in the market and therefore hotel values.

With the improvement of the security situation and the lifting of travel warnings, the Nairobi hotel's market should gradually recover. By ensuring a peaceful presidential election, the country would regain the international community confidence, and that's all that is needed. The values dropped by 6.4% in 2016, accounting for a massive amount of new supply that impacted the level of occupancy. However, HVS is confident that strong economic growth combined with the introduction of international brands into the market and a steady growth in demand will allow Nairobi to experience a significant increase in room values when the excess of supply is absorbed.

For detailed analysis visit http://hvi.hvs.com/market/africa/Kenya_-_Nairobi

BUSINESS & FINANCE

HVS Africa Market Summary by Country

Mauritius

With blue waters and wonderful climate, Mauritius is one of the dream tourist destinations on the Indian Ocean.

Mauritius registered 1,150,000 tourist arrivals in 2015, which translates into an 11% increase from 2014. South African Airways has further strengthened its routes to Mauritius due to growing demand – both from the continent and internationally.

Mauritius recorded double-digit increases in occupancy although in US$ terms RevPAR was down around 25%, in local currency there was an impressive 12% increase. The long term future for the island is positive with the government growing the economy in different sectors, all of which will need hotel accommodation. In addition increased airlift direct from Europe should sustain demand for the resorts. Announced new hotels include Park Inn by Radisson in Quatre Bornes, the new commercial hub of Mauritius.

Mauritius is a mature and established market that does not need to prove itself anymore. Tourists displaced by terrorism are likely to visit Mauritius. It will suffer from the rising competitiveness of other peaceful and sunny destinations (Cape Verde, Seychelles, etc). The values are expected to drop by 0.5% in Mauritian Rupees terms but will be stable in US dollars terms although far below the peak level reached in 2016.

For detailed analysis visit http://hvi.hvs.com/market/africa/Mauritius

Morocco

Morocco has been one of the better performing political and economic countries in the North African region. According to Trading Economics, Morocco's GDP grew from a paltry 1.8% in January 2015 to a respectable 4.5% at the end of the year. This stellar performance can be attributed to a stable economic environment and an established tourism industry. The WTTC reported Morocco's tourism industry contributed 7.7% to the country's GDP in 2015 and is projected to grow by 4% between 2016 and 2026.

Casablanca

Casablanca on the other hand has also seen a drop in performance, albeit more marginal than for Marrakech. Occupancy fell slightly and ADR was flat in local currency terms.

Casablanca may not experience the same recovery situation. The fear of terrorist attacks combined with economic uncertainty and the lack of attractive new supply will push the occupancy and rates down, producing a 6.9% drop in REVPAR. Yet, the additional income from the various in-house F&B facilities will help keep the values at a stable level of US$135,000 per room, although still lower than the pre-crisis level. The 186-room Four Seasons Hotel Casablanca has opened, marking Four Season Hotels and Resorts' second property in Morocco.

For detailed analysis visit http://hvi.hvs.com/market/africa/Morocco_-_Casablanca

Marrakech

Marrakech had a tough year in 2015 with falls in both occupancy and ADR, resulting in a fall in RevPAR of 21%. France remains a key market for the country as a whole so the increased terrorism in France and general nervousness surrounding North Africa, meant many tourist chose not to travel to the country.

Morocco presents a mixed picture for 2016. Holiday makers are coming back to Marrakech but the political push leads to economic nervousness and uncertainty. Marrakech should see a drop of occupancy owing to the amount of supply entering the market at a bad time for tourism. Luckily, the introduction of new branded four-star hotels may boost the average rates up and the security situation should encourage the clients to stay in the hotels extensively and thus increase F&B facilities revenue. This will trigger an increase of 10.3% in values in Moroccan Dirham. However, due to the currency devaluation following the economic uncertainty in the country, the values per room should drop by 7.6% in US dollars terms.

For detailed analysis visit http://hvi.hvs.com/market/africa/Morocco_-_Marrakech

Namibia - Windhoek

Namibia's economy is integrally linked to that of South Africa and the rest of Southern Africa. Based on this consideration, the same headwinds that are faced by South Africa will have an impact on the Namibian economy, with low growth prospects being the order of business. Sluggish global demand and low prices for its key commodities exports will continue for the foreseeable future.

The outlook for tourism in Namibia remains bright, as it is boosted by incredible natural attractions. The government is actively involved in supporting and marketing the country to source markets through several international offices. The Department of Environment and Tourism coordinates tourism legislation and is supported by such bodies as Namibian Tourism Board, the Federation of Namibia Tourism Association, Hosea Kutako International Airport, Ministry of Home Affairs and Immigration. Hotel performance in Windhoek broke with a three-year growing trend in 2015 with a drop in occupancy, although it remains well ahead of historic levels. There was an impressive 8% growth in ADR in local currency. Hilton Worldwide has announced the signing of a management agreement with Out of Africa Hospitality to open a mid-market Hilton Garden Inn hotel in Windhoek, Namibia. The new property will open adjacent to the existing Hilton Windhoek in 2017. In US$ hotel values remain strong, although the trend has fallen due to the currency fluctuation. After a slow start to the year Windhoek experienced a rebound in tourism in 2016. Occupancy reverted back to previous level, close to 70%, with an increase in average rate in line with the high inflationary level in the country. REVPAR and hotel values increased by 12.9% in Namibian dollars terms.

For detailed analysis visit http://hvi.hvs.com/market/africa/Namibia_-_Windhoek

BUSINESS & FINANCE

HVS Africa Market Summary by Country

Nigeria

Nigeria is one of the countries that were most adversely affected by the commodities and currency crises. The country has not reported a single case of Ebola since the crisis was declared over, however Boko Haram has not yet been brought under complete control.

Abuja

Total international tourist arrivals in 2015 did not exceed 2014 levels, however Nigeria has a larger domestic tourism market. Abuja hotels saw an increase in occupancy in 2015 despite the Boko Haram insurgency. Average room rate did not perform as well with a substantial decrease from $325.00 to $275.00. Like Lagos, this is due in large part to the lack of international guests and an increase in local guests. Many new hotels are planned for Abuja over the next five years, which illustrates the confidence in which the market is held for the longer term. Accordingly, both Lagos and Abuja experienced reduced hotel values, however these reductions were less severe than 2014.

Abuja is struggling to regain the confidence of tourists and investors. The fall in prices of gas and oil slowed the economy down in 2016, security is a massive concern for travelers and the accessibility to both cities is not improving. The level of demand and occupancy is expected to be down. Hence, Abuja will see a drop in values of 2.1%, suffering from a massive drop in occupancy. The improvement of the security situation and the economic recovery will partly condition the future of the hotels investment playground in Nigeria.

For detailed analysis visit http://hvi.hvs.com/market/africa/Nigeria_-_Abuja

Lagos

In 2015 Lagos experienced an increase in occupancy compared to 2014 although below historic levels. Unfortunately the change in focus to domestic travelers has resulted in a sharp fall in ADR. STR Global analysts cite Boko Haram conflicts in the country as well as uncertainty during the Nigerian general elections and low oil prices as negative factors contributing to Lagos' overall performance.

The long term remains positive with Carlson Rezidor announcing the signing of its first Quorvus Collection in Africa: the 5-star, 244-room luxury Emerald Grand Hotel & Spa in Lagos, Nigeria.

Lagos is struggling to regain the confidence of tourists and investors. The fall in prices of gas and oil slowed the economy down in 2016, security is a massive concern for travelers and the accessibility to both cities is not improving. The level of demand and occupancy is expected to be down, although Lagos should be less impacted owing to its position as capital. The hotels' value in Lagos is expected to rise by 2.5% thanks to a rise in average rate and REVPAR. The improvement of the security situation and the economic recovery will partly condition the future of the hotels investment playground in Nigeria.

For detailed analysis visit http://hvi.hvs.com/market/africa/Nigeria_-_Lagos

Seychelles

With blue waters and wonderful climate, the Seychelles is one of the dream tourist destinations on the Indian Ocean. Seychelles has seen much political turmoil after it earned its independence from Britain. However, since a political coup d'état took place in the mid 1980s, the country has not looked back.

Seychelles has won a tourism attraction award, the Most Scenic Holiday award at the International Travel Expo (ITE). Besides marketing aggressively in the Indian Ocean countries such as India, Dubai, UAE and many others, Seychelles is achieving success in such western countries as Brazil and others in South America.

Hotel trading performance in 2015 was encouraging with stable occupancy and growth in RevPAR. This, despite the islands having to secure new sources of business in recent years and now focusing more on the Asian markets. HNN has shared the encouraging view that "Chinese travelers are arriving in larger numbers; the island enjoys some of the highest room rates in the world; more than 2% of arrivals come via private plane"

The Seychelles hotel industry has seen an increase in hotel values of 4.6% in 2015. 2016 was a good year for the Seychelles hotel industry; values grew by 8.2% owing to a 5% growth in demand and a 3% growth in rates.

The archipelago remains a luxury destination that has been able to re-invent itself and open up to new source markets along the path. It will definitely benefit from the economic growth of Sub-Saharan countries. The value per room will reach its peak since 2011, at US$538,000.

For detailed analysis visit http://hvi.hvs.com/market/africa/Seychelles

BUSINESS & FINANCE

HVS Africa Market Summary by Country

South Africa

South African Tourism, the marketing wing of the government's Department of Tourism, continues to perform an important function of keeping the country top of mind when it comes to holidaymakers and business travelers. The Home Affairs Department has eased the new entry visa regulations that had such a negative impact on visitor numbers in 2015. The currency exchange rate has had a positive impact on tourism numbers and these are expected to rise even further. Brexit raises fresh concerns for the tourism market in South Africa, given the large number of British tourists who visit the country. Uncertainty over their economy at home and the weakening of Sterling may deter many from long haul trips.

Cape Town

Cape Town saw a small dip in occupancy to 66%, but ADR (in US$) remained steady, despite the weakening of the Rand against the US$. In local currency there was a 30% growth in ADR. This represents four consecutive years of strong performance, proving the oversupply is fully absorbed. This is further illustrated by Tsogo Sun Group starting construction on a 500-room hotel complex comprising three brands in Cape Town. There is a planned development at the Capetonian Hotel in Heerengracht; and the Gorgeous George Hotel and Bar development being constructed in St Georges Mall. All these hotels are located in the central business district.

Also benefitting from the currency exchange rate, the Cape Town hotel market will keep performing well in 2016. The REVPAR will increase by 6.7% thanks to a peak in occupancy and a strong rate growth. Values will reach their highest level at US$167,000. Victim of its own success, Cape Town will need to deal with an increasing amount of supply coming into the market in the next few years which might affect hotels' performance and value until this oversupply is absorbed.

For detailed analysis visit http://hvi.hvs.com/market/africa/South_Africa_-_Cape_Town

Durban

Durban is the only Commonwealth country city that agreed to play host to the 2022 Commonwealth Games. Preparations have started with the announcement of many commercial projects. Durban hotel performance was more or less in line with that of the other two South African cities we are covering with growth in both occupancy and ADR.

Hotel values in South Africa rose impressively in 2015 in Rand terms, due to a steady increase in revenue per available room. However, in dollar terms the country has not done so well, with a 16% drop in value for Johannesburg and Durban in 2015. Cape Town bucked the trend with only a marginal decrease in US$ terms. This performance is consistent with the currency crisis that was evident throughout all the emerging market economies.

Durban is still a growing market with strong occupancy growth combined with a 12% increase in ADR in 2016 will lead to an 18.7% REVPAR increase. With a low amount of supply coming in and a growing demand, the hotels' performance is expected to keep growing at a steady pace. In line with the two big other South African cities, Durban benefit from the exchange rate and the increase in value is 29% in 2016.

For detailed analysis visit http://hvi.hvs.com/market/africa/South_Africa_-_Durban

Johannesburg

Johannesburg enjoyed the highest level of occupancy for at least six years and strong ADR performance, with RevPAR growing by 16% in local currency. Unfortunately the performance of the Rand against the US$ masks this strong growth.

Marriott has announced plans to construct a flagship hotel at the Melrose Arch, which is a popular mixed-use development providing a live, work and play environment outside the central business district.

Johannesburg has seen a peaceful transition of power in 2016 that helps regaining corporate and investor's confidence. The hotel industry in Johannesburg should benefit from the advantageous exchange rate of the Rand. Hotel's performance is expected to show a positive trends and hotel values would rise by 14.4% in Rand terms and 24.3% in US dollars.

For detailed analysis visit http://hvi.hvs.com/market/africa/South_Africa_-_Johannesburg

Tanzania - Dar es Salaam

Landlocked Uganda has announced it will build a major pipeline to export its oil through Tanzania. This is seen as a major source of confidence in Tanzania's stability and safety profile. From this major infrastructure investment Tanzania can generate more FDI and capitalise on the benefits of a subsidised route for its own oil. Dar es Salaam saw a 12% increase in room supply in 2015, unsurprisingly occupancy fell significantly. The 2015 elections will also have affected demand.

However, positively there was a substantial increase in ADR in local currency, pushing RevPAR up almost 7%. A 20% fall in value of the Shilling against the US$ results in a fall in value in the HVI, although it should be noted in local currency terms there was a noticeable increase in value. Any worsening of the security situation and accessibility are major threats for the future of Dar es Salaam hotel industry. Yet, corporate travelers and overnight tourists waiting to fly to more touristic destinations are coming in and international brands start entering the market. Although the additional supply will impact the occupancy level, the average rate will be boosted by a strong inflation and the introduction of four-star branded hotels in the city. The values are expected to grow by 4.1% in 2016, after three years of bad performance owing to the currency devaluation against the US dollar.

For detailed analysis visit http://hvi.hvs.com/market/africa/Tanzania_-_Dar_es_Salaam

BUSINESS & FINANCE

HVS Africa Market Summary by Country

Togo - Lome

327,000 visitors from far and wide enjoyed the wonders of Lome in 2013. With tourism contributing 3.1% to the GDP of the country, the tourism market remains underdeveloped. Most of the major infrastructures are inadequate and the roads' network is deficient in the capital.

Togo has a limited and uneven hotel supply. In 2012, rated hotels represented 900 rooms and 6 units in Lome. Accor Hotels and Carlson Rezidor are the only international brands operating in the city. In addition to the international chains, Group Onomo and Grupo Prefaco opened 2 hotels in Lome in 2014. Most of the hotels in Togo are state owned, although it's now changing as the government wants to sell them to private investors. The government does not invest in any refurbishment or renovations, and does not have any hospitality expertise, leaving the properties outdated and under-performing. The on-going process of decentralization should encourage private investors and boost the premium travel accommodation supply in the country.

However, behind this layer of negativity, Lome has a real potential to grow its tourism activity. The level of occupancy had been stable since 2011, showing a rebound in 2015. ADR and REVPAR have been significantly up reaching a peak of +18.2% in REVPAR last year, boosted by the newly opened international hotels attracting demand from international travelers. Hotel values have thus experienced positive and encouraging trends, with double-digit growth over the two last years.

Investors are increasingly considering Togo for investment. The inflow of Foreign Direct Investment increased by 61% in 2013 and 49% in 2014. Despite overall positive trends, Lome still needs to address key challenges to be able to develop. In addition to the poor infrastructure, hotels in Lome tend to be overpriced, compared to the product offering and airline fares are dissuasive for travelers.

Although Lome faces some challenges in growing the tourism market, it offers economic and political stability. The city is expected to see positive trends in 2016. The opening of the Radisson Blu will trigger induced demand and help in catching the tourists and investors' interest. Thanks to the low amount of supply, mid-size conferences such as AHIF (June 2016) can have a significant impact on the occupancy level. Hotels' values are expected to rise by 8.2% in 2016, reaching a peak value of US$125,000.

For detailed analysis visit http://hvi.hvs.com/market/africa/Togo_-_Lome

Zambia - Lusaka

The copper mining industry in Zambia has impacted the economy of Zambia in the same way other emerging markets whose economies are supported by commodities. As an alternative strategy at maintaining economic growth, Zambian authorities are looking at the tourism industry. Initiatives such as the Zim-Zam UniVisa and the eVisa are targeted at increasing tourist arrival figures by simplifying movement across African countries

The Zambian Investment Agency expressed optimism that the country was able to capture the targeted 1 million tourist arrivals in 2015. According to the Zambia Tourism Board (ZTB), Zambia received more than 946,000 tourists in 2014, Zambia Airports Corporation Limited reported 1.36 million arrivals in 2012, with international visitors accounting for 1.14 million, illustrating current levels are significantly below historic numbers. The Chinese are still regarded as a prime source of tourists into Zambia and will continue to be targeted.

Performance of hotels in Lusaka was relatively stable in 2015 with a marginal increase in occupancy and a small drop in room rate. As a result hotel values in Lusaka fell only slightly in 2015 (-2.6%), compared to a massive drop in 2014 (-12.4%). Companies clearly view this as a short term problem as Hilton Worldwide has announced the development of a brand new Hilton Garden Inn which is targeted to open in 2017 and Quantum Global purchased the Intercontinental Hotel Lusaka from Kingdom Hotel Investments.

Benefitting from a stable amount of hotel supply, Lusaka is expected to see the hotels' occupancy and average rate reasonably grow. The sale of the Intercontinental in 2016 demonstrated investors' confidence and boosts values up to US$142,000, representing a 6.8% growth against 2015.

For detailed analysis visit http://hvi.hvs.com/market/africa/Zambia_-_Lusaka

Zimbabwe - Harare

Known as "a world of wonders" in Southern Africa, Zimbabwe welcomes more than two million tourists a year, Although tourism contributes 10.4% to the GDP of the country, the tourism market remains underdeveloped. Most of the major infrastructures are outdated and roads need to be upgraded. Political unrest and violent strikes shake the country and many Zimbabweans have left their homeland. Hotel supply has not grown for the past five years and is mostly made of local unbranded properties that struggle to adapt to the needs of international tourists. Harare lacks international hotel brands which would bring quality and expertise to the current tourism landscape. However, the country has a real potential to grow its tourism activity. The level of occupancy has been increasing since 2014, proving a rebound in demand from international tourists. While ADR and REVPAR are down, owing to the competitiveness of bordering countries, the picture may change quickly. Indeed, global hospitality brands have started showing interest in the nation. Carlson Rezidor recently announced the opening of a Radisson Blu Hotel in Harare in 2019, and it will certainly encourage competitive brands to enter the market.

Investors are increasingly considering Zimbabwe for investment. Capital investments are expected to rise by 4.8% per year over the next ten years. China is being a precious ally: President Xi Jinping confirmed multi-billion investments in energy and infrastructure and the cancellation of US$40 million in debt in exchange of the yuan becoming Zimbabwe's international currency. This should push the number of business tourists from China in need for a hotel room. The government will need to tackle significant challenges in the next few years to be able to take advantage of this increasing demand, get the ADR back to previous level and boost hotels' values on the market. Harare will be significantly impacted by the political and economical crisis in 2016. The demand goes primarily to Livingstone and the Victoria Falls, but the corporate guests are not keen to visit Harare at the moment bringing occupancy down. The 6% deflation significantly impacts the average rate. Hotels' values are expected to drop to their lowest level since 2010, at US$104,000, representing a 17.6% decrease.

For detailed analysis visit http://hvi.hvs.com/market/africa/Zimbabwe_-_Harare

CONSERVATION

A Ranger's View On RHINO POACHING

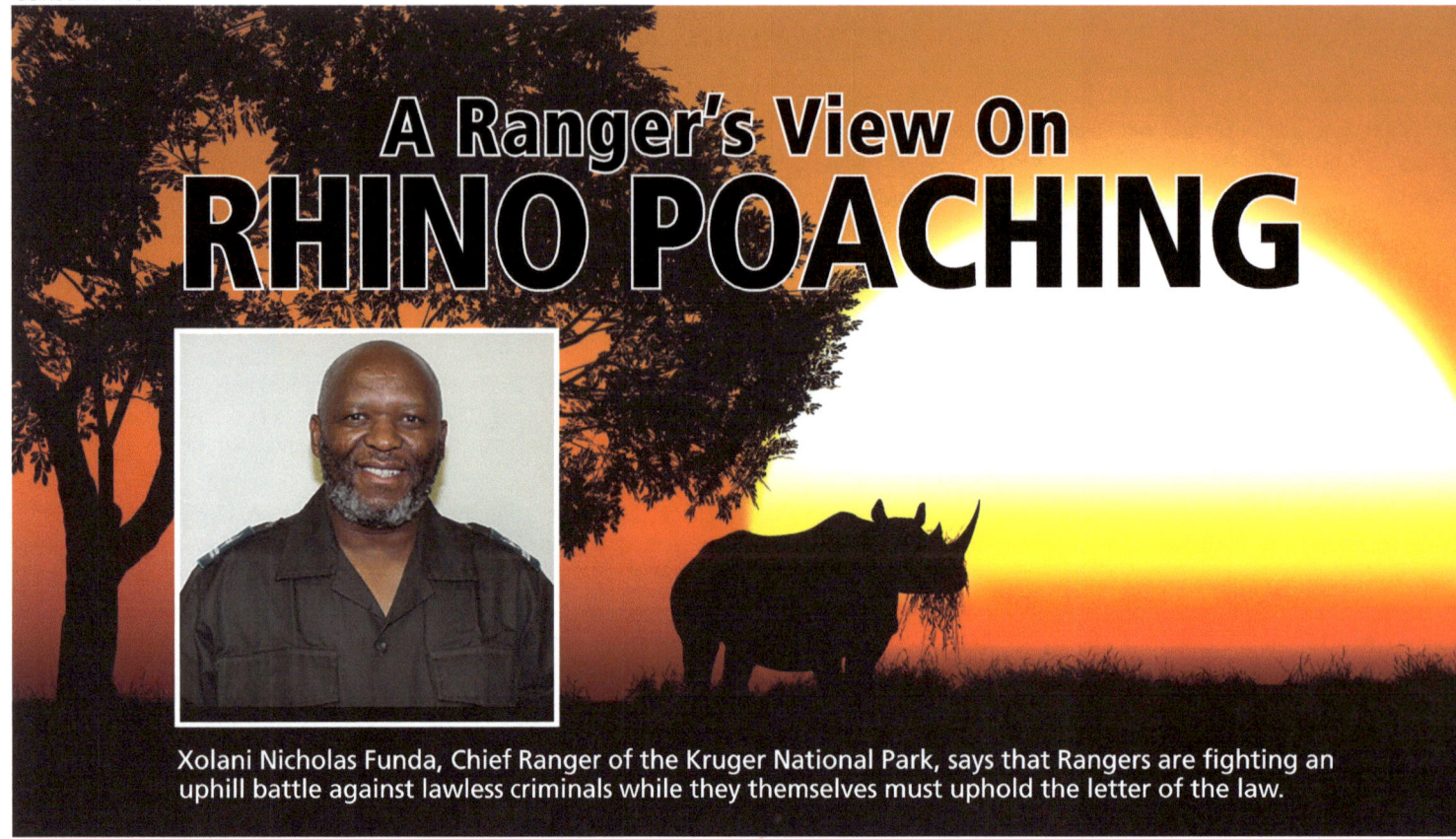

Xolani Nicholas Funda, Chief Ranger of the Kruger National Park, says that Rangers are fighting an uphill battle against lawless criminals while they themselves must uphold the letter of the law.

Leading counter-poaching operations have always been part and parcel of a ranger's responsibilities. There has been a massive surge in rhino poaching across Africa in recent years as a result of well-organised poaching syndicates targeting this iconic species for their own economic gains. Threat levels have thus escalated and Africa's rangers are increasingly involved in armed skirmishes on a daily basis.

The Game Ranger's Association of Africa (GRAA) reports that rangers working in the Kruger National Park (KNP) refer to it as 'the beast'. "With a size of 19 485km² and temperatures that soar to a blistering 50°C, working in the field is not for the faint-hearted. Rangers work up to 21 days in the bush under these harsh conditions, without the luxuries many of us take for granted, and away from their families and loved ones." With the Kruger alone losing up to three rhinos a day, rangers are operating on a 24/7 basis, being pushed to their limits by this savage onslaught that is rhino poaching.

Funda confirms that rangers become familiar with the animals of the area on their daily patrols, and develop an attachment to these animals. "When you see a rhino lying peacefully in the bush, you wish sometimes you could chase it away to a place where no one will find it and it cannot be harmed," says Funda. When rangers find a blood bath of a butchered rhino in their section they lose a part of themselves.

Operating in this environment demands constant vigilance, even withholding information from fellow staff to prevent any leaks. The threats do not always come from beyond the fence. Funda begrudgingly acknowledges, "The value of rhino horn is encouraging people to get involved in things they never thought they would get involved in." This was illustrated in 2016 when respected section ranger Rodney Landela and vet technician Kenneth Motshotso were caught for rhino poaching.

The GRAA published that Landela had been in the KNP's service for 15 years and received several Achievement Awards. "It cannot be denied that there are people who are willing to cross the line between good and bad, right and wrong; but the field rangers of KNP who arrested their superiors must be applauded for doing what is right and for dedicating their lives to protecting our natural heritage," confirms the GRAA.

Poor people are cheap and rangers are law abiding citizens

Rhino poaching is an issue that goes far beyond the frontiers of conservation. It is an issue of socio-economic standards of the country and national security.

When one doesn't have anything to eat, one is not inclined to prioritise respecting natural resource conservation. The truth is that until poverty is resolved in South Africa, particularly in areas surrounding reserves, syndicates will have a pool of poor people to recruit and poaching will continue. For the desperate man trying to feed his children, the financial reward he receives in exchange for rhino horn is an offer he is rarely able to resist.

Rangers continue to risk their lives protecting defenceless animals, despite their limited power against the ruthless poacher who is equipped with state of the art weapons and who has no regard for human or animal life. Funda disagrees with people who refer to this poaching crisis as a war. "It will only be a war once it is declared as such by the President." War implies the rules of battle are used by both parties. Poachers are criminals that are not guided by rules. Rangers, however, are governed by the law and respect South Africa's constitution, which enshrines the rights of all people in South Africa and affirms the democratic values of human dignity, freedom and equality. Should poachers be injured in the bush, rangers ensure these criminals receive the necessary medical care. Fighting poaching is, at times, very restrictive.

The Game Rangers Association of Africa works closely with reserves like the KNP to ensure rangers are continuously receiving specialised training to better equip and empower themselves to make informed decisions during conflict situations. Some of these courses include the Protected Areas Security Operations Planning (PASOP), Advanced Field Ranger Training and Counter Insurgency Tracker Training (CITT) and the Use of Force.

A ranger's heart

The Kruger is divided into 22 sections, with designated section rangers and field rangers per section. Operating under these conditions takes

CONSERVATION

its toll on the rangers' wellbeing. On their daily patrols, rangers become familiar with the animals of the area and develop an attachment to certain animals, knowing where to find them and where their preferred grazing areas are. "When you see a rhino lying peacefully in the bush, you wish sometimes you could chase it away to a place where no one will find it and it cannot be harmed," says Funda. When rangers find a blood bath of a butchered rhino in their section they lose a part of themselves. Poachers are also starting to take the ears and tails of poached rhinos. This has already happened in a number of cases in the KNP – whether the muti trade is jumping on the bandwagon is still open for debate. Such scenes are immensely debilitating for the ranger who has committed his/her life to the conservation of wildlife.

The Chief's toolbox

Kruger's anti-poaching unit and rangers are continuously raising their game to ensure they are prepared for poachers' ever-changing tactics. Dogs, helicopters, firearms, motorbikes and night vision equipment are just some of the tools within Chief Ranger Funda's toolbox. Funda notes that these tools are all working very well in this battle, "but nothing will be able to replace my ranger."

While Funda's position has elevated to Chief Ranger, his heart is still with the rangers working in field. Funda is not in the field as much as previously, which means he is able to enjoy warm meals and a soft bed to sleep on. However, he never forgets the ranger in the field that has sacrificed everything, knowing they can be killed in the bush by ruthless poachers, all to protect South Africa's wildlife. One thing is certain in these terrible poaching times – field rangers are an irreplaceable force.

Rhino Conservation Awards

The Rhino Conservation Awards, held annually since 2012 to celebrate those that continue to fight rhino poaching, will be held on 21 August, under the patronage of Prince Albert II of Monaco. The Awards were founded by Dr. Larry Hansen and Miss Xiaoyang Yu, are sponsored by ZEISS, and held in collaboration with the South African Department of Environmental Affairs and the Game Rangers Association of Africa.

There are five categories: Best Field Ranger, Best Conservation Practitioner, Best Political, Investigative and Judicial Support, Best Rhino Conservation Supporter, and Special Award for Endangered Species Conservation.

For more information visit *www.rhinoconservationawards.org*

Rhino Poaching Deaths vs Poacher Arrests - Stats for South Africa by Province

Year / Deaths vs Arrests	2010 Deaths	2010 Arrests	2011 Deaths	2011 Arrests	2012 Deaths	2012 Arrests	2013 Deaths	2013 Arrests	2014 Deaths	2014 Arrests	2015 Deaths	2015 Arrests	2016 Deaths	2016 Arrests	2017 Deaths	2017 Arrests
KNP (SanParks)	146	67	252	82	425	73	606	133	827	174	*826	*317	458	177	??	??
MNP (SanParks)	00	00	06	00	03	00	03	00	00	00	00	00	00	00	??	??
MAP (SanParks)	00	00	00	00	00	00	00	00	01	01	00	00	00	00	??	??
Gauteng	15	10	03	16	01	26	08	10	05	21	00	00	00	00	??	??
Limpopo	52	36	80	34	59	43	114	34	110	60	12	00	30	00	??	??
Mpumalanga	17	16	31	73	28	66	92	00	83	45	02	04	14	00	??	??
North West	57	02	31	21	77	32	87	70	65	14	00	03	15	00	??	??
Eastern Cape	04	07	11	02	07	00	05	26	15	02	00	00	13	00	??	??
Free State	03	00	04	00	00	06	04	07	04	00	00	00	03	00	??	??
KwaZulu-Natal	38	25	34	04	66	20	85	63	99	68	06	01	51	00	??	??
Western Cape	00	02	06	00	02	00	00	00	01	01	00	00	00	00	??	??
Northern Cape	01	00	00	00	00	01	00	00	05	00	00	00	05	00	??	??
*Unofficial											*329	*107	*596	*237	*1068	??
TOTAL	333	165	448	232	668	267	1004	343	1215	386	*1175	*432	*1054	414**	*1068	??

KNP = Kruger National Park, MNP = Mpumalanga National Park, MAP = Mapungubwe National Park. *Source: StopRhinoPoaching.com **Statistics released by the DEAT as at 11 Sep 2016. Regular updates from DEAT were discontinued in 2015.

Incidents of poaching can be reported to the anonymous tip-off lines 0800 205 005, 08600 10111 or Crime-Line on 32211.

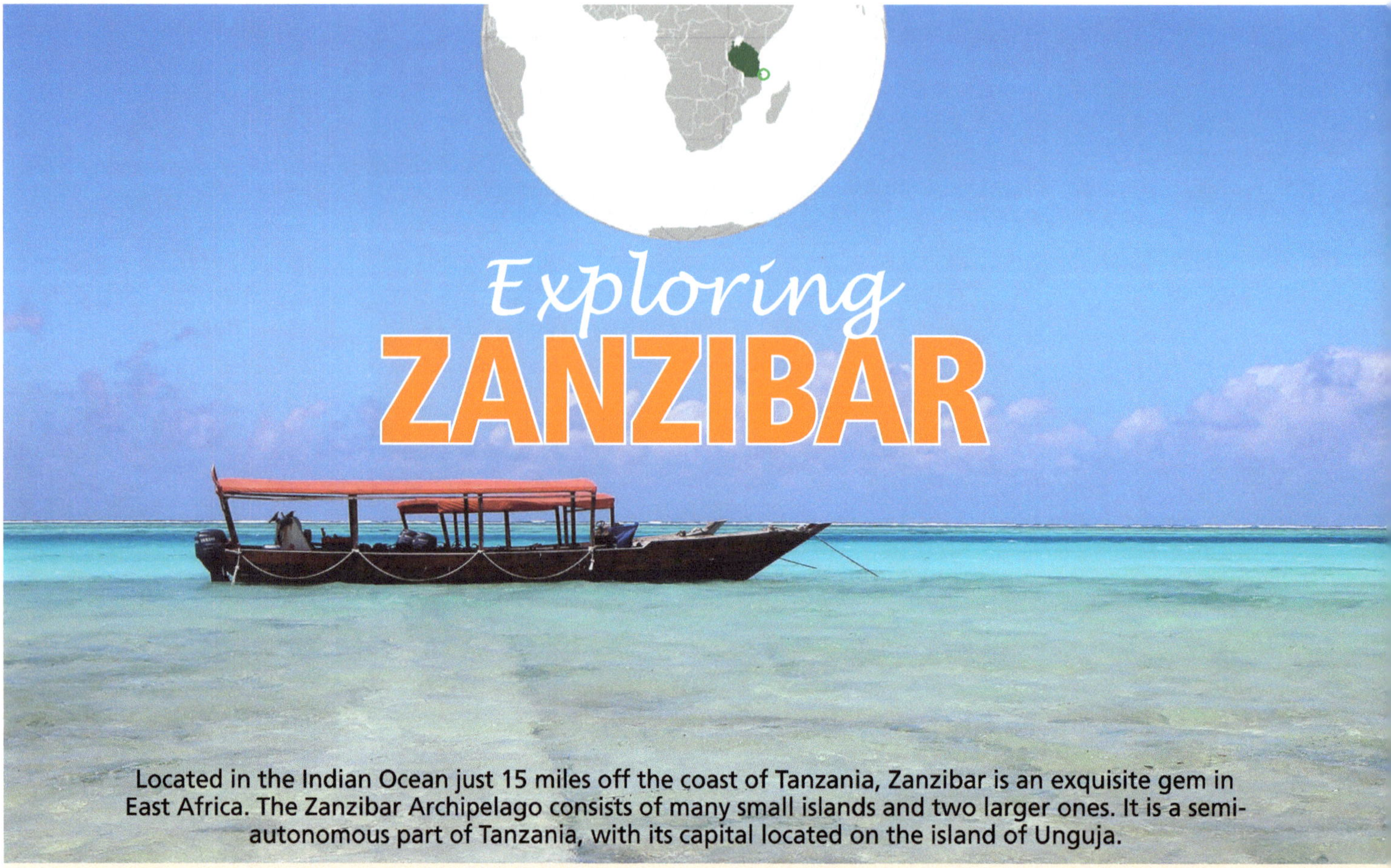

DESTINATIONS

Exploring ZANZIBAR

Located in the Indian Ocean just 15 miles off the coast of Tanzania, Zanzibar is an exquisite gem in East Africa. The Zanzibar Archipelago consists of many small islands and two larger ones. It is a semi-autonomous part of Tanzania, with its capital located on the island of Unguja.

There is much to see and do in Zanzibar, whether you are looking for an adventure, a touch of history or just pure relaxation. Zanzibar's scenic landscape is second to none and is home to unique wildlife found nowhere else in the world. Is Zanzibar your next escape? Here are 5 splendid to-do activities that you should add to your travel itinerary!

True to its name, Prison Island is a former prison for slaves and a quarantine station fro Zanzibar. Strategically located just off the Old Stone Town, Prison Island offers more than its notorious history. It is also home to giant land tortoises known as the Giant Aldabra Tortoise. These large creatures were previously imported from the island of Seychelles in the 19th century and have made Prison Island their home ever since.

Giant Aldabra Tortoises can live up to 2 centuries long and is an herbivorous animal, eating grass, leaves and woody plant stems. Take the opportunity to feed and pet these gentle giants when you take a stroll along Prison Island!

Get Up-Close & Personal with Endangered Animals

Zanzibar is also home to some of the world's most endangered animals including the red colobus monkey and the servaline genet. The Zanzibar red colobus monkey can be found on some islands of the Zanzibar Archipelago including the larger island of Unguja. Like most primates, they are a social species living in troops between 15-30 animals. The Zanzibar red colobus is the most endangered monkey species in Africa, with a population estimate of between 2,000 to 3,000 individuals.

Another endangered species found in Zanzibar is the Zanzibar servaline genet. You'd be interested to know that this subspecies of the servaline genet was only recently discovered and named in 1995! Live Zanzibar servaline genets were first photographed in 2003, allowing for new information about the genet to be documented. As of yet, its conservation status is still unknown.

Both these endangered species can be found at the Jozani Chawka National Bay Park on Unguja Island. Due to its close proximity to mainland Tanzania, travelers usually combine a Tanzania & Zanzibar safari trip to be able to catch a glimpse of these small animals in the wild!

Explore Nungwi & Kendwa Beaches

Ask travelers what they think is the top thing to do in Zanzibar and most would probably say to visit the islands' many beaches. Famous for its powdery white beaches and protective barrier reef that line its Eastern coastlines, beaches in Zanzibar are second to none. There are many beaches to choose from should you go exploring but Nungwi and Kendwa beaches are the most popular choices among locals and tourists.

Nungwi beach is located north of the island and is unique because it doesn't experience significant low tides, allowing swimmers to

swim all day without having to chase the waves all the way out into the ocean. Another popular beach is Kendwa beach, located south of Nungwi. Kendwa is Nungwi's quieter counterpart, boasting a lesser crowd and a more relaxed atmosphere. Kendwa is the perfect place to just sit back, relax and perhaps enjoy a relaxing dose of yoga or even an exhilarating surf experience while you watch the sunset!

Satiate the Taste Buds

It is only fair that island life comes with it a scrumptious selection of fresh seafood! Find yourself indulging in the freshest seafood available in Zanzibar at the Forodhani market. This marvelous nighttime food market opens its doors to hungry foodies in the late afternoon. At the market, you will find yourself spoilt for choice as you indulge in row after row of grills filled with fish, prawn, lobster, crab and squid. This is street food at its best – inexpensive and delicious. But as with all street food, do exercise caution and choose only the freshest ingredients. Pay attention to the chef who is preparing your food to ensure good hygiene.

Indulge in a Spice Tour

It is almost unthinkable to leave the island also known as "Spice Island" without going on a spice tour. In the 19th century, Zanzibar was known as one of the world's leading producers of a variety of spices including nutmeg, cinnamon and clove. Initially introduced by Portuguese traders to the island in the 16th century, modern day Zanzibar still produces high quality spices that are exported internationally.

On your spice tour, you will see how spices are cultivated, experience first hand their smell and taste and get the opportunity to buy some locally grown spice home! The vibrant colors of the spices are definitely as much a feast for the eyes as it is for the taste buds and a great photo opportunity to share with family and friends. Perhaps you might also be inspired to cook up a storm in the kitchen!

For more information visit www.bookallsafaris.com

EVENTS

EVENTS

8 Reasons to Attend THINC Africa

30-31 Aug 2017 Cape Town

If you missed the inaugural Tourism, Hotel Investment and Networking Conference (THINC) Africa event last year, then you do not want to miss the second conference taking place at the FNB Portside Building in Cape Town's iconic V&A Waterfront precinct in August. Here's 8 valid reasons why you should attend.

By **Des Langkilde**.

1. Made for Africa.

Expertly tailored by HVS, and benefiting from their expertise in hosting premier hotel investment conferences globally, THINC Africa is becoming THE key conference in this part of the globe.

2. Look Who's Talking.

Top hotelier and hospitality expert speakers, including developers and both debt and equity funders. Here's some name dropping: Adrian Gardiner (Chairman, Mantis Collection); Tim Smith (Managing Director, HVS Cape Town), Stephen Claassen (Provincial Head, FNB), James Vos (Shadow Minister of Tourism), Mike Collini (VP Development SSA, Hilton Group), Roeland Vos (CEO, Belmond), Dimitris Manikis (VP Business Development, RCI Europe, Middle East and Africa), and a lot more.
Click here for a full list of names.

3. Industry Relevant Topics.

The final programme is still being developed, but so far topics include: Launch of the HVS Hotel Valuation Index; Finance and other challenges in Africa; Leaders' Session; Alternative Hotels; Global Hotel Market and Values; The Evolution of Management Contracts; Debt Session; HR / Educational Session; Round Table Sessions – Countries: Kenya, Mauritius, Mozambique; Improving Customer Experience; How to attract International Tourists. Click here to download the agenda.

4. Networking.

This two-day event is expecting 200 delegates, up from last year's 160, thus providing ample opportunity to network with peers and business contacts, allowing delegates to discover new and exciting opportunities in this fast expanding market.

5. Look, Listen, Learn and Engage.

Delegates will leave the conference having been challenged and learned something new. Audience participation is encouraged so delegates can have their questions and issues addressed. Speakers are instructed to 'not be boring or say something that can be Googled' – people want opinions.

6. Investment Opportunities.

Discover and explore investment opportunities and options in various territories on the African Continent (including Mauritius, Seychelles and Mozambique).

7. Increase Revenues.

Opportunities for growth on the African continent mean that hoteliers can generate great revenues to benefit themselves and local communities.

8. Recognition.

The inaugural THINC Africa Awards will honour and recognise the most outstanding hotels, general managers and students in Africa. The awards are open to nominees throughout Africa and the nomination forms are available on THINC Africa. Click here to enter the awards.

And finally, you'll get to meet me! As an official media parter to THINC Africa 2017, TourismTattler will be covering the event – who knows, you may be mentioned in our media broadcasts.

For more information visit www.thincafrica.hvsconferences.com

HOSPITALITY — PROPERTY REVIEW

TOWN LODGE Midrand
By City Lodge Hotels

Location and convenience are the prime motivators for city hotel selection in business tourism. This pearl of wisdom occurred to me when checking into the City Lodge Midrand.

By **Des Langkilde**.

Before setting off on my business trip to attend The Hotel Show Africa, I searched the web for hotels positioned as close as possible to Gallagher Convention Centre in Johannesburg, South Africa. And City Lodge Hotel Group's website provided the answer – Town Lodge Midrand.

With a wide range of accommodation options to choose from, the Group's hotel brands Fairview, Courtyard, City Lodge, Town Lodge, and Road Lodge, are clearly displayed with each brand featuring its hotel locations by city with rates (there's a significant saving for booking online compared to walk-in rates). Note though, that you have to select Midrand and not Johannesburg from the 'Choose Hotels by City' booking dropdown menu.

As my flight was scheduled for a late Sunday evening departure to Johannesburg, being able to simultaneously book a night at City Lodge Hotel at OR Tambo International Airport was certainly convenient as the hotel is a short walk from the arrivals concourse along the parking block opposite the airport.

After a sumptuous breakfast on Monday morning (their buffet spread is a sight to behold), I checked out and set off for the Gautrain station, which again is a short walk from the hotel along the airport concourse.

Gautrain is an 80-kilometre mass rapid transit railway system in Gauteng, which links Johannesburg, Pretoria, and Ekhuruleni to the airport. The trains run from 05:15 am to 09:20 pm and depart every 10-15 minutes during peak hours. After recharging my Gautrain Gold Card, I caught the Sandton bound train, jumped off at Marlboro station, and boarded the Pretoria bound train which I disembarked at Midrand – the next station along the route. The entire trip took under 30 minutes, which is amazing when compared to two hours that the same trip would have taken to navigate through Jo'burg's traffic congestion by taxi.

I then caught the Noordwyk bound Gautrain bus from Midrand station using my Gold Card (cash is not accepted on these buses) and jumped off at the 2nd stop along Old Pretoria Road, almost opposite the Gallagher Convention Centre.

After a tiring day attending presentations at the Vision Conference, which formed part of the Hotel Show Africa, I summoned an Uber ride to my hotel. Thankfully, Town Lodge Midrand is only a 6-minute drive away and I was relieved to be allocated a smoking room on check-in.

The rooms at Town Lodge are somewhat smaller compared to City Lodge rooms, but I found mine to be comfortable with all of the requisite needs of a business traveller catered for, including complimentary WiFi and a writing desk. With 118 rooms in the hotel, my room just happened to one of the two rooms designed to meet the special needs of the physically disabled, which was rather convenient as they're positioned on the ground floor close to the reception, sundowner bar, and dining room. There's even a vending machine for snacks and beverages just down the passageway.

I was curious about the linen change card provided in the room, so after another typically sumptuous breakfast the following morning I met the hotel General Manager, Shelley Steel for a coffee and chat sitting around the pool deck. Ms. Steel tells me that she's been with the City Lodge Group for 20 years, so when she says that guests appreciate eco-friendly initiatives and tend to opt for re-using the same linen to save water, she made me embarrassed as I'd forgotten to place the card on my bed.

My perception that Town Lodges are frequented by business travellers was confirmed when Steel said that their occupancy is 80% during week days. "Our weekend occupancy is somewhat lower but with the Kyalami motor racing track being close by and the new Mall of Africa being built near Midrand, we are seeing an increase in leisure tourists."

I asked why Town Lodge is rated 2-Star by the TGCSA when the rooms and amenities are clearly 3-Star. "We had a total refurb done between 2014 to 2016, and although Town Lodge does meet 3-Star criteria, the Group management decided to stay with the lower rating to better differentiate between the brands," said Steel.

Before heading off to attend another grueling day at Gallagher, I popped into my room to ensure that my conscience would sleep better that night.

For more information visit www.clhg.com

FROM THE BENCH™
With Louis the Lawyer
BENCHMARK ©

The Consumer Goods & Services Ombudsman

Part 1
IMPLICATIONS FOR THE TOURISM INDUSTRY

WHO OR WHAT IS THE CONSUMER GOODS & SERVICES OMBUDSMAN ('CGSO'), WHAT ARE THE IMPLICATIONS, AND WHAT MUST THE TOURISM INDUSTRY DO?

The office of the Consumer Goods & Services Ombudsman ('CGSO') was established (early 2015) in terms of section 82 of the Consumer Protection Act 2008 (Act No. 68 of 2008) ('the CPA').

Succinctly the purpose of the CGSO ombudsman is the following:

- Guide Industry – set minimum standards of conduct re engaging with Consumers AND assist in resolving Disputes;
- Raise the standards of conduct;
- Offer Guidance re compliance CPA and fair business practices;
- Educate Consumers as to their rights and redress;
- Provide for a scheme of alternative dispute resolution such as mediation.

The CGSO Code of Conduct ('the Code') is enforceable against Consumer Goods & Service Industry Participants – who are the latter?

The easiest way to explain this is to list the relevant definitions that appear, bearing in mind that any definitions, words and phrases used will have the same meaning as in the CPA:

'*Consumer Goods and Services Industry*' means all Participants involved in the Supply Chain that provide, market, offer to supply Goods and Services to the Consumer, unless excluded in terms of 4.4 hereof (i.e. if they are subject to another ombudsman e.g. Banking).

'*Participant*' means any entity operating within the Industry.

'*Supply Chain*' is defined in the CPA as follows:

'supply chain', with respect to any particular goods or services, means the collectivity of all suppliers who directly or indirectly contribute in turn to the ultimate supply of those goods or services to a consumer, whether as a producer, importer, distributor or retailer of goods, or as a service provider (thus includes intermediaries such as travel agents & tour poperators).

It's mandatory for all Participants to do the following:
- Comply with provisions of the Code;
- Register with CGSO as per the procedures provided on the CGSO website from time to time;
- Contribute towards the funding of the CGSO;
- Establish internal complaints-handling process;
- Monitor complaints;
- Display on its trading premises the CGSO decal and on their website a prescribed notice that states they are Participants to Code and bound by it;
- Make a copy of Code and/or summary thereof and its internal complaint-handling procedure available to any Consumer upon request;
- Ensure staff and agents have adequate knowledge of CPA, Regulations issued, Code and internal complaints-handling procedure – this means that training of the CGSO and CPA per se is crucial and must be ongoing;
- Keep records for 3 years of the Complaints received and recording that a Consumer was referred to CGSO for assistance in resolving; details of the Complaint, including details such as nature, time involved, whether it was resolved and if so the remedy provided/ not resolved;
- Such data must be used by the CGSO to highlight recurring complaints, be shared with management, staff, and Industry;
- Behaviour to resolve Complaints and Disputes must be in accordance with the law, the spirit and provisions of this Code and the CPA – the reference to 'the spirit' is important e.g. do not exclude liability for gross negligence in your T&C and/or indemnity and hope no-one will notice!

The CGSO will determine a strategy for conducting awareness and education of the Code and contents thereof by introduction and/or facilitation and/or distribution of information brochures, guidelines and workshops, and guidance regarding compliance particularly aimed at smaller Participants via workshops, website, etc.

Disclaimer: *This article is intended to provide a brief overview of legal matters pertaining to the tourism industry and is not intended as legal advice. © Adv Louis Nel, 'Louis The Lawyer', July 2017.*